Volume 9

MODERN FIGHTING AIRCRAFT

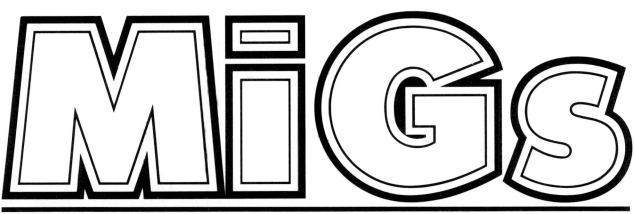

Published by Arco Publishing, Inc.

New York

A Salamander Book

Credits

Published by Arco Publishing Inc.,
215 Park Avenue South,
New York, NY 10003,
United States of America.

© Salamander Books Ltd., 1985

All correspondence concerning the content
of this book should be addressed to
Salamander Books Ltd.,
Salamander House, 27 Old Gloucester Street,
London WC1N 3AF, United Kingdom.

This book may not be sold outside the
United States of America and Canada.

Library of Congress Cataloging in Publication Data
Sweetman, Bill.
MiGs.

(Modern Fighting Aircraft; v. 9)
"A Salamander Book."
1. MiG (Fighter planes) I. Title. II. Series.
UG1242.F5S95   1985   623.74'64   85-5966
ISBN 0-668-06493-5

Project Manager: Ray Bonds

Editor: Bernard Fitzsimons

Designed by Grub Street Design, London

Jacket: Terry Hadler

Cutaway drawings: © Pilot Press Ltd.

Line and colour artwork: © Pilot Press Ltd.;
and Mike Badrocke, Keith Fretwell, Terry
Hadler, Stephen Seymour, TIGA, Mike Trim
and Tudor Art © Salamander Books Ltd.

Filmset by SX Composing Ltd.

Contents

Acknowledgements

Author

Anyone seeking to write about Soviet
aircraft must trawl every source with a
fine net. A full set of references for a book
such as this would probably be half as
long as the book itself, and it would be
invidious to select specific examples.
However, *Air International, Flight
International,* the *Interavia* publications
and *Aviation Week & Space Technology*
were extensively farmed for the
information in these pages.

The author would like to extend a
particular word of thanks to Richard
Ward of General Dynamics for advice,
encouragement and help in navigating
the sometimes perilous waters of this
subject.

The publishers are also grateful to all
those who contributed photographs,
particularly Bill Green, Malcolm
Passingham and the US Department of
Defense.

Bill Sweetman is Western USA
correspondent for the Interavia Group,
contributing extensively to *Interavia,
International Defense Review* and
Interavia AirLetter. Between 1973 and
1979 he was on the staff of *Flight
International*, where as well as covering
the air transport industry he launched
the 'Flight Intelligence' series of detailed
technical analyses of modern Soviet
military aircraft, including the first
accurate descriptions published of
'Backfire', 'Foxbat' and 'Flogger'. From
1979 to 1981 he was Air Correspondent of
the national Sunday newspaper, *The
Observer*, before moving to California.
His books include *A Concise Guide to
Soviet Military Aircraft* (Hamlyn/
Presidio, 1982), as well as contributions
to the Salamander titles *Soviet Air Power*
(1978) and *Air Forces of the World*
(1979), and an earlier volume in this
series, *A-10 Thunderbolt II* (1984).

Colour reproduction by Rodney Howe Ltd.

Printed in Belgium by Proost International Book Production, Turnhout

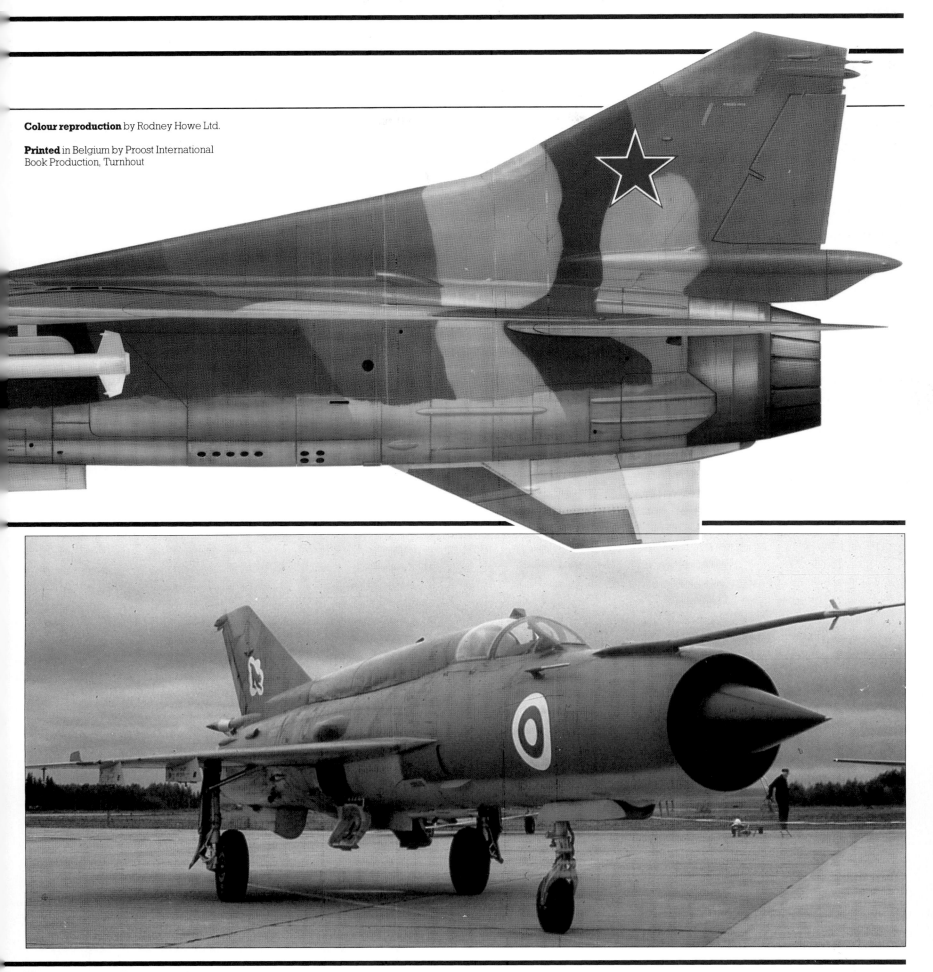

Introduction

For most people, the word "MiG" is purely and simply synonomous with a Soviet fighter. Not literally true, this reflects the fact that the vast majority of Soviet fighters in the jet age have stemmed from the design bureau named after Artem Mikoyan and Mikhail Guryevich.

Soviet warplanes are seldom described with any accuracy in the West. They are portrayed as highly capable threats, comparable to the best of the West's fighters, when it is time to make defence plans and draft budgets; but when the astronomical unit costs of Western systems have to be explained to the public, the Soviet fighter is depicted as a crudely designed and rudely constructed agricultural implement.

If there is one central theme in this book, it is that MiGs are neither Porsches nor wheelbarrows. Rather, they are fighting machines designed to rigidly utilitarian standards, many of them set by factors which do not apply or are not considered important in the West. Another difference is that many of the criteria by which the Soviet Union's planners assess the merits of an aircraft design can be applied equally to a tank, ship or missile system.

It is from the world of armour that the author's favourite parable about the differences between Soviet and Western design practices is drawn. In the course of the Eastern campaign of World War II, the Wehrmacht captured one of the Red Army's deadly T-34 tanks and shipped it back to one of the German manufacturers for assessment. The engineers' response, in essence, was that they could never build a T-34 because it would not pass their quality control inspection. The rest is history.

The Bureau and the System

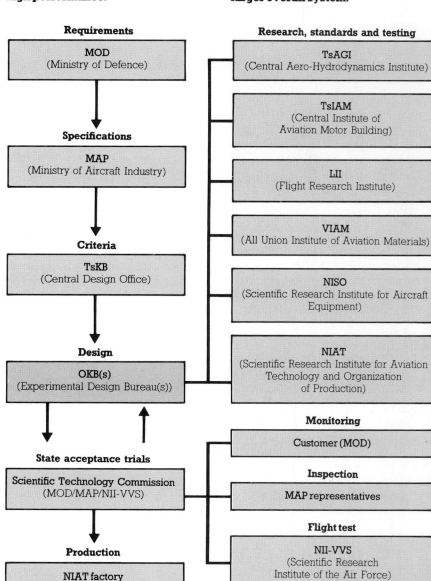

Soviet designers work in a completely different environment from the familiar Western system, and some understanding of the differences is essential if Soviet design philosophy is to be understood. The Soviet designer's job is to respond to a specification drafted by the unified Soviet armed forces, using a comprehensive set of standards and guidelines developed by the Soviet industry over the years. The Mikoyan-Guryevich bureau rose to prominence through the design of the MiG-15, MiG-17 and MiG-19, rugged, uncomplicated fighters that exactly met the armed forces' demands.

No Westerner can be unaware that the affairs of the Soviet Union are managed differently from those of the United States, Britain or France, but it is sometimes difficult to appreciate just how deep those differences run. In historical perspective, the Russian Empire had barely emerged from feudalism before 1917, when the rule of the Tsars collapsed. Attempts at Western constitutional democracy had been made, but their effects were superficial. Politically, the vast domain of the Romanovs was an unpolluted culture, a laboratory-clean environment for the first experiment in Marxism.

Post-revolutionary Russia, and the Union of Soviet Socialist Republics established in 1922, was not the first society to be governed according to a set of writings and precepts, or in which decisions and laws were made by the interpretation of such principles. A great many theocracies – countries ruled by a religion and its priests – have existed throughout history, and some still do. Marxism, however, is not a religion. Marxists regard it as a scientific theory applying to all the workings of society.

Most aviation books do not start with a discussion of political doctrine. In Western terms, it is out of place. But in dealing with the development of Soviet military aircraft, some reference to the importance of Marxism is not merely relevant; it is essential.

Very often, new Soviet weapons have been over-rated or under-estimated in the West, and to a startling degree. Examples of this have included the MiG-21, which was regarded as virtually useless until it started taking a heavy toll of 'superior' US Air Force fighters over Vietnam. In the case of the MiG-25 the reverse was true: US analysts greatly overestimated its performance. The latter error cost the American taxpayer dearly, because the exaggerated threat was fed into the design of the F-15 fighter and substantially increased its size and cost.

In both cases, Western observers could not resist the temptation to draw direct parallels between Soviet and Western aircraft. Given that East and West are equally subject to the laws of mechanics and aerodynamics, this can be valuable. When it is a matter of requirements, goals and design priorities, it can be grossly misleading; it has sometimes been called 'mirror-imaging'. Its root cause is the failure to put the weapon in the right context.

Constant references to the teachings of the Communist party, and the presence of political officers and functionaries at all levels, are not just the outward trappings of a one-party state. They are real fundamental guidelines in all

aspects of endeavour. The relationship between the industrial managers, the military, the technologists and the Party is not a one-way affair; successful people in all walks of life tend also to be influential in the Party.

There are no exceptions to the rule of Party and doctrine. The process by which Soviet aircraft are brought from the requirement stage to the front line, and the way in which they would be used in action, are fundamentally affected by such considerations. At every phase, decisions are made in accordance with larger principles of 'military art' or 'technical art' which apply to all military operations, or to the design of all military vehicles. These principles, in turn, are founded not only on experience and experimentation, but also on doctrine.

According to Western observers and Soviet defectors, the core of power in the Soviet Union is the Defence Council, a group within the Politburo that encompasses the Party, the armed forces and, probably, the KGB. The position of the aircraft industry reflects that structure. It is entirely geared to meeting the needs of a single 'customer' – the Ministry of Defence (MoD), from which all aircraft requirements and specifications emanate. Commercial aircraft, too, are built to military standards, and would be used for airlift tasks in wartime; the effect of military requirements can be seen in many features of their design, some of which are inexplicable in commercial terms.

The MoD is the administrative head of the Soviet armed forces. These are unified to an extent which is almost incomprehensible in the West, where, for instance, the US Army, Navy and Air Force will debate roles, missions and funding among themselves at the highest level. In the Soviet Union, resources and responsibility are divided along functional lines.

A warning should be entered at this

Above: First design from the MiG bureau was the MiG-1, a high-altitude fighter whose stubby lines indicated a concern with weight reduction and high performance.

Below: This simplified chart of Soviet procurement procedures shows the central place of the experimental design bureau (OKB) within the much larger overall system.

Requirements	Research, standards and testing
MOD (Ministry of Defence)	**TsAGI** (Central Aero-Hydrodynamics Institute)
Specifications	**TsIAM** (Central Institute of Aviation Motor Building)
MAP (Ministry of Aircraft Industry)	**LII** (Flight Research Institute)
Criteria	**VIAM** (All Union Institute of Aviation Materials)
TsKB (Central Design Office)	**NISO** (Scientific Research Institute for Aircraft Equipment)
Design	**NIAT** (Scientific Research Institute for Aviation Technology and Organization of Production)
OKB(s) (Experimental Design Bureau(s))	**Monitoring**
	Customer (MOD)
State acceptance trials	**Inspection**
Scientific Technology Commission (MOD/MAP/NII-VVS)	MAP representatives
	Flight test
Production	**NII-VVS** (Scientific Research Institute of the Air Force)
NIAT factory	

Left: Artem I. Mikoyan, photographed in March 1966. Aged 34 when the MiG bureau was founded, he headed it until he literally died at his drawing board in 1970. The status and influence of leading Soviet engineers such as Mikoyan is almost unbelievable in Western terms.

Right: "For Stalin!" reads the legend on this MIG-3 interceptor, assigned to the defence of Moscow. Even in 1942, MiG fighters were distinguished by cowling bumps and bulges.

Below: MiGs were not the most distinguished of Soviet wartime fighters. This MiG-3 has fallen into German hands, and its base has been taken over by Bf 109s.

Right: These MiG-3s seem to be split into elements of three, with lead aircraft and wingmen distinctively marked. Rigid tactics compensated for expertise lost in pre-war purges.

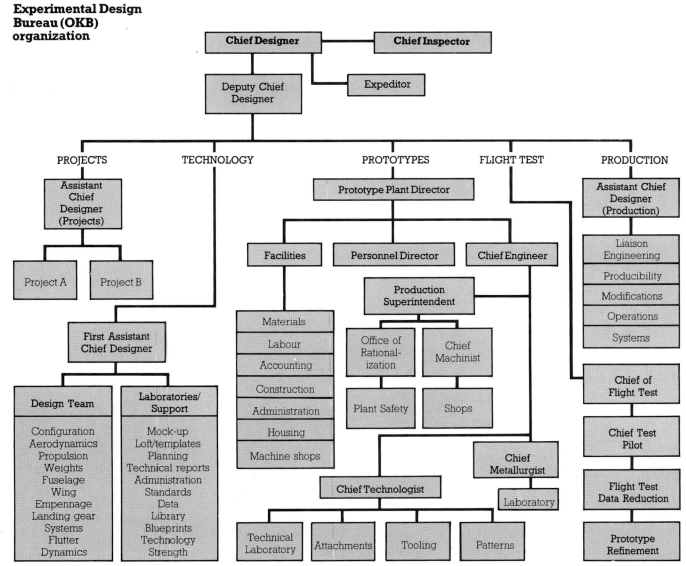

point: in the early 1980s, it became apparent in the West that many components and relationships within the Soviet military organization had been changed, but by late 1984, the precise details of the changes had not been identified. What follows is based on the 1984 assessment by the International Institute of Strategic Studies.

The casual observer of the Soviet military may get an impression of a Western-type structure, because an organization named the 'Soviet Air Forces' (VVS) does exist under the MoD. However, the VVS lacks one vital element of an independent force: it does not command its assets in combat. In the case of tactical fighters and strike aircraft, the VVS is responsible for supplying, training and supporting some 25 large combat units, some described as Regional Commands and some designated as Air Armies. The majority of the aircraft produced by the Mikoyan bureau serve with these formations. Up to 1983, these forces were generally referred to as Frontal Aviation (FA), and were all designated as Air Armies; however, the FA designation appears to have been abandoned.

For military operations, these units are commanded by an entirely separate hierarchy, reporting to the MoD. As far as is known, the vast Soviet tactical forces are divided into three main theatres, each aligned in a direction of critical interest: the Western theatre faces NATO, the Southern deals with the Middle East and Afghanistan, and the Far Eastern theatre stands opposite China and the Far East. The Western theatre, which is the largest, is believed to be subdivided into three smaller 'theatres of military operations,' or TVDs. The Regional Commands and Air Armies are assigned to the theatres or, in the Western theatre, the TVDs.

The structure reflects the Soviet view that fighting units are for combat, and should be burdened as little as possible

with support tasks such as logistics, maintenance and training. It is also significant that the operating VVS units are not necessarily under the command of ex-pilots – as it happens, most TVD commanders have risen through the land forces, while tactical air officers find promotion in the VVS; even so, a TVD commander is expected to think like one, not like an armour or motor-rifle type.

Below: The OKB is a compact organization, with its own design, prototype manufacture and flight test facilities. A 'skunkworks' operation is an approximate Western parallel.

Experimental Design Bureau (OKB) organization

Chief Designer	**Chief Inspector**
Deputy Chief Designer	**Expeditor**

PROJECTS — TECHNOLOGY — PROTOTYPES — FLIGHT TEST — PRODUCTION

Assistant Chief Designer (Projects)

Project A — Project B

Prototype Plant Director

Facilities — **Personnel Director** — **Chief Engineer**

Assistant Chief Designer (Production)

Liaison Engineering
Producibility
Modifications
Operations
Systems

First Assistant Chief Designer

Design Team	**Laboratories/ Support**
Configuration	Mock-up
Aerodynamics	Loft/templates
Propulsion	Planning
Weights	Technical reports
Fuselage	Administration
Wing	Standards
Empennage	Data
Landing gear	Library
Systems	Blueprints
Flutter	Technology
Dynamics	Strength

Materials
Labour
Accounting
Construction
Administration
Housing
Machine shops

Production Superintendent

Office of Rationalization — **Chief Machinist**

Plant Safety — Shops

Chief Technologist

Technical Laboratory — Attachments — Tooling — Patterns

Chief Metallurgist

Laboratory

Chief of Flight Test

Chief Test Pilot

Flight Test Data Reduction

Prototype Refinement

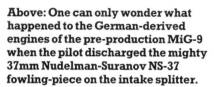

Above: One can only wonder what happened to the German-derived engines of the pre-production MiG-9 when the pilot discharged the mighty 37mm Nudelman-Suranov NS-37 fowling-piece on the intake splitter.

Another difference between the VVS and a Western air force is that its tactical fighters are assigned only to the defence of military targets in the theatre of operations. The defence of the Soviet Union itself is the task of a different organization, Voyska-PVO (National Air Defence Troops), which encompasses interceptors, surface-to-air and anti-ballistic missiles, and the command, communications, warning and control systems without which they would be useless. PVO formations are assigned to specific targets and regions, and vary in size according to the importance of the target and its vulnerability to attack; the largest single PVO command is the Moscow Air Defence District. The PVO is the other user of MiG designs.

PVO reorganization

In the major reforms observed in the early 1980s, the main effect on the PVO was the removal of virtually half its fighter aircraft. The loss was not as great as one might think, though, because the aircraft eliminated were older types which could hardly expect to catch a B-52, and would have no chance at all against a B-1. The older aircraft were transferred to the VVS, and are assigned to the theatre commands, as auxiliary interceptors and reserves.

In their respective fields, the VVS and PVO are responsible for training, including the development of tactics. They are responsible for ensuring that their sys-

Above: Most MiG-9s had a more conventional armament installation. Not the prettiest of fighters, the type made the most of low-thrust engines.

tems are able to defend against the threat where needed, and to carry out their missions in the face of defensive systems. They are responsible for maintenance and reliability, and must ensure that their weapons will be available to execute their missions.

One important feature of Soviet procurement in the past has been the fact that the PVO and VVS have presented fundamentally different requirements, not only in terms of weaponry, avionics and flight performance, but also in terms of maintenance levels and base specifications: the difference is as great as that between the USAF and US Navy. There is currently a trend towards common equipment, but it may yet reverse.

A third organization may now be issuing requirements for combat aircraft: the construction of a true aircraft carrier on the Black Sea indicates that a new generation of naval fighters must be under development, with requirements being developed by the AVMF (Soviet Naval Aviation). Apart from this specialized and secret endeavour, all require-

ments for new fighters start at the headquarters of the PVO or VVS.

In the case of a major development programme, one that is expected to lead into production, the MoD's decision is likely to be made – or at least approved – at Politburo level. Both MoD and Politburo decisions will take very similar factors into account. In the Soviet system, money is not central to the economy; since virtually the entire legal economy is governed by the state, the flow of money from the public to the private sector and back again, the factor which determines most Western budgets, is negligible. Instead, decisions are taken in terms of resources. The MoD considers whether to expand missile production, or whether to increase its capacity for building combat aircraft. Again, it may advise doing both, but this could mean using labour, factory space and mater-

Above: The MiG-15UTI – known under the NATO reporting system as 'Midget' – was the standard trainer for Soviet fighter pilots for decades until the introduction of the Aero L-39. This example was photographed after being overhauled in Prague for the Iraqi Air Force, which used the type into the late 1970s.

Right: This Czech-built CS-102 (MiG-15UTI) featured an Izumrud search radar, and probably had a reserve role as an interceptor. In the 1950s, Warsaw Pact allies were permitted to build such aircraft.

ials that could have been used to build airliners (earning relatively hard cash from the Warsaw Pact) or even consumer goods.

Strategic decisions of this sort must be considered by the Politburo. There are limiting factors involved in the allocation of resources to the MoD, as opposed to other users. The most important concern such things as agriculture, energy, raw materials and communications – the infrastructure without which the MoD cannot function. There is also a minimum standard of living to be considered, below which the people will be neither healthy nor trustworthy. The Defence Minister, as the head of the MoD and a member of the Defence Council, sees such decisions from both sides. Once the decision is made, the Politburo will hand it down to the Council of Ministers – in theory the Soviet Cabinet, but in fact the Politburo's administrative staff – for execution by the Ministry of Aircraft Industry (MAP).

This process has a fundamental impact on the design of Soviet aircraft. A

Below: This MiG-15bis, in bright red and pale blue colour scheme, was used by the Moskovsky Okrug PVO aerobatic display team – the Red Falcons – and flown at early Aviation Day demonstrations in the mid-1950s.

Above: Under Project Moolah, the USA offered asylum and money to any pilot defecting with a MiG-15. The project was successful, and analysis and testing of the MiG-15 helped to define tactically important modifications to the F-86 Sabre, such as the importance of the all-moving "flying tail" for high-speed pitch control. (See below for original markings.)

requirement for a new tactical fighter, for instance, will be framed by the VVS in terms of the threat it will face, the targets which it will be expected to attack, and the development of tactics at the theatre and tactical level. Its costs (in terms of resources) and merits will be assessed by the MoD, and weighed quite objectively against the needs of other branches of service. If it is considered a priority, and the Politburo has made sufficient resources available to the MoD, the industry will be asked to fill the requirement – but that is the industry's first official involvement in the process.

Requirement pull

The result is that Soviet aircraft developments are the result of what is called 'requirement pull': the service has a requirement, and once it is approved the industry directs its technical and industrial resources to meet it. Western military aircraft, on the other hand, are more often defined by 'technology push'. The industry carries out research and predicts the performance and characteris-

tics of future weapons using new technology; the military reviews the potential of the technology, and selects for development those weapons which offer the greatest military advantage.

This distinction can illuminate many of the differences between Soviet systems and Western systems, and the way in which they are developed and introduced to the fleet. For instance, a requirement-pulled procurement system tends to be driven by the threat, as well as by offensive military objectives. There is an inevitable lag between the time that Western plans become clear, or the time that a Soviet strategy change is made final, and the fielding of a system that responds to such a development. In some cases, this explains why the Soviet Union appears slow to introduce one new technology, while it is very quick to field another.

Technology that does not respond directly to the needs of the user will usually be bypassed, or left to a later generation. The importance of this lies in the fact that the user is the TVD or

theatre commander. His first priority is numerical strength; Soviet military doctrine stresses the fact that the stronger force starts with an advantage. In the case of aircraft, producibility times reliability equals availability, or the number of aircraft ready to be flown against the target at any time.

Defining objectives

When the TVD commander needs a major improvement – the ability to extend conventional bombardment behind the battlefield, to implement a change in strategy or to counter improvements in the threat – what Soviet texts call 'military-technical art' will be employed to provide it. But from the commander's perspective, an improvement in any given performance number – an increase in range, turn rate, radar detection range or transonic acceleration – is not significant unless it meets a specific objective at a higher level. It does not of itself justify a replacement of an existing type, and will be cheerfully traded for easy production.

An excellent example of this mechanism in action is the development of lookdown, shoot-down (LDSD) radar/missile systems. The first of these was tested in the USA in the late 1950s, long before the Soviets had low-altitude, all-weather offensive aircraft in service. Such aircraft were still not in the Soviet inventory when the AWG-9/Phoenix LDSD system was first ordered into production, in the early 1960s. That is a case of 'technology push'. The Soviet Union did little about LDSD capability until the number and importance of low-altitude, adverse-weather penetrators in the Western arsenal began to climb, in the early 1970s. In the later years of that decade, an interim LDSD system entered Soviet service, and testing of full-capability systems surged ahead, in a classic example of 'requirement pull'.

The task of the MAP – the Ministry of Aircraft Industry – is to respond to the requirement. Essentially, MAP is the Soviet aircraft and engine industry. It embraces production, design, development and basic research, together with the control of standards and specifications. Its organization, however, makes it less of a monolith than its size might imply.

Most of MAP's facilities and personnel are spread among its large subdivisions.

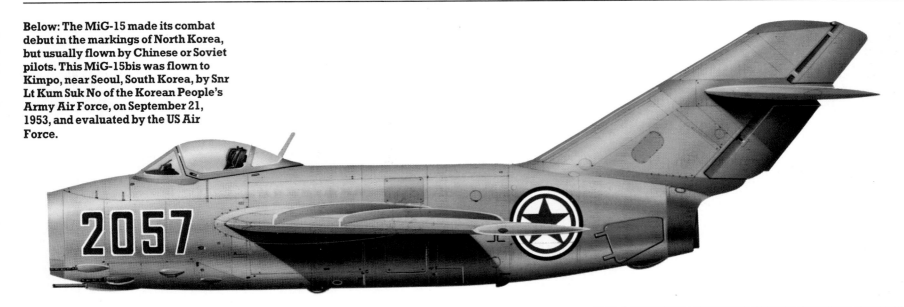

Below: The MiG-15 made its combat debut in the markings of North Korea, but usually flown by Chinese or Soviet pilots. This MiG-15bis was flown to Kimpo, near Seoul, South Korea, by Snr Lt Kum Suk No of the Korean People's Army Air Force, on September 21, 1953, and evaluated by the US Air Force.

Four of them are each associated with one discipline of aircraft design: aerodynamics, engines, avionics and systems, and materials. Another is responsible for advanced flight research. To that extent, these divisions of MAP constitute a Soviet equivalent of the National Aeronautics and Space Administration, but they are much more than that. The propulsion and the avionics/systems organizations include the design offices, for one thing. For another, they do not merely provide data for the aircraft designers, or conduct research in support of aircraft programmes, but directly influence the way aircraft are designed. The results of their research are summarized in manuals and technical memoranda, and issued as guidelines to the engine and airframe designers. They cover many basic aspects of design; most of the combat aircraft in Soviet service have planforms and air inlet designs which were centrally defined and selected in this way.

One complete division of MAP is responsible for manufacturing technology, and the maintenance and equipment of State Aviation Factories (GAZ). This organization carries out its own research into ways of making aircraft easier to build – reducing the number of parts, using new processes to eliminate scarce or costly materials, making assembly sequences easier – and, no doubt, issues its own guidelines to the designers.

Also under MAP is an organization with no Western equivalent: the Central Design Bureau (TsKB). The role of the TsKB is highly influential in the evolution of Soviet aircraft, because it is the means by which the advantages of competition, and the incentive to build a better product, are introduced into the planned, quota-dominated world of industry.

The TsKB carries out many of the functions of a Western company's advanced-design department. When a requirement is submitted to MAP, it is the TsKB which carries out the feasibility study and determines what sort of aircraft will be needed to meet it; what sort of new technology will have to be incorporated in the structure, engines and avionics; and, ultimately, whether the requirement can be met and with what resources. In the process, it collaborates with the other MAP divisions and draws on their specific expertise. Once the initial studies are complete, and approved

by the military customer, the TsKB passes its work on to another set of organizations: the design bureaus.

What makes the TsKB most unusual in the Soviet structure is that it heads a group of organizations which, often, compete with one another. These are the Experimental-Design Bureaus, or OKBs. Despite its title, an OKB is more than a design office; it is a substantial organization, capable of designing an advanced combat aircraft, building a number of prototypes, and – with the assistance of the MAP's flight-test department – carrying out the complete development programme. It also oversees preparations for production. The largest OKBs can handle multiple programmes.

OKB constraints

The OKBs are not autonomous. Their task is to interpret a fairly tight specification laid down by the TsKB, and produce a prototype which responds to it. They interpret that specification in accordance with the standards set by the other MAP organizations, and design to incorporate components – engines, avionics, ejection seats and so on – available from those organizations. The design task is probably simpler and quicker than starting from scratch.

In the past, the TsKB has often instructed two OKBs to build prototypes, with the better one being selected for production. Alternatively, on occasion, a single OKB has built two prototypes sharing common components, but with a different basic layout. More recently, there has been less evidence of such 'fly-off' contests, probably because they take up a great deal of time and materiel. (One factor which facilitates fly-offs in the West – the fact that manufacturers will usually provide competing prototypes below cost, in hopes of future profits after they win - does not apply in the Soviet Union.) However, paper designs and computer simulations are undoubtedly still compared.

To talk about 'competition' is, perhaps, not quite accurate, and 'comparison' may be a better word. The OKBs, unlike Western design teams, do not depend on winning contests for their survival; some of them have remained active for many years without designing a production aircraft, and have even won awards for the usefulness of their work. (Take Kamov as an example. Only two produc-

tion designs, and one derivative, have emerged from Kamov in the past 30 years, but the bureau has pioneered many useful helicopter technologies.) Under whatever name, the process gives the TsKB a choice of approaches to its requirement.

To the Western eye, the MAP may look like a vast bureaucracy, within which progress would be impossible. However, there are a number of features which make the system work more smoothly than one might expect. The staffs of the different organizations are very stable, and lines of promotion are

Above: A radar-equipped MiG-17PF 'Fresco-D' interceptor on final approach. The intake bullet houses the conical scan search element of the Izumrud radar, and the bulged lip contains the ranging set. The large area of the wing is apparent.

Below: This Shenyang FT-5 (Chinese two-seat trainer version of the MiG-17PF), photographed at its Pakistan AF base in March 1981, illustrates the generally high quality of workmanship apparent on most of the south-of-the-border 'bootleg' MiG designs.

Above: A North Vietnamese MiG-17F under attack by US Navy F-8 Crusaders on December 14, 1967. In such low-level engagements subsonic speed was no handicap.

Below: This high-altitude reconnaissance photo – quite possibly taken from a U-2 or a drone – shows two MiG-17Fs at Phuc Yen, 20 miles northwest of Hanoi, in October 1966.

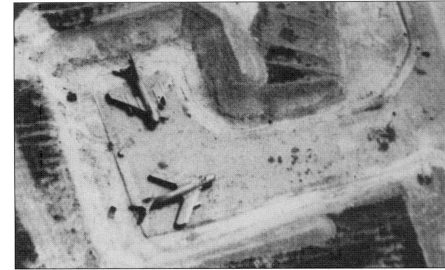

Above: Two MiG-17Fs maintain an unnervingly close formation on an Il-18 transport. Not the fastest fighter in service at that time, the late 1950s, the MiG-17 was still the standard Soviet fighter-bomber.

Below: Possibly taken at the Mikoyan OKB's home near Moscow, this photo shows two service MiG-17Fs climbing away, and a gaggle of variously marked MiG-19PMs, along with one MiG-17F, in the background.

clear and mostly vertical. The result is that, firstly, the individuals within the system have a great deal of experience in their specific jobs; and, secondly, that working relationships between individuals are of very long standing. The Soviet system contrasts sharply with most Western organizations. Consider Britain, where virtually none of the Civil Service policy-drafters with access to the Cabinet level has any background in engineering, or take the case of the USA, where programmes are managed by serving officers who are promoted and transferred every couple of years.

Stable cross-departmental relationships can be accommodated within the Soviet system, because there is no contractor/customer relationship involved, so issues of 'conflict of interest' do not arise. People within the MAP aerodynamics, engine, systems and production organizations are even assigned to, and work alongside, the designers of a specific OKB for years at a time. The designer faced with a problem may not have to submit a memorandum in triplicate to the MAP production branch. Instead, he walks three doors down and discusses the problem with the production-branch representative in the bureau, with whom he has worked for five years. It may not always work that way, but it works better than Western foes of socialism might care to admit.

OKBs are not lightly formed or disbanded in these days, but that was not always the case. Many OKBs, now unknown, were formed and fell under Stalin; some major bureaus of their day simply vanished before the mid-1950s. Most of today's leaders, however, were operating in the years before the 1939-45 war – or the 1941-45 war, as it should properly be termed in discussions of the Soviet Union – and rose to prominence during the war years. They included Yakovlev, Ilyushin and the only design bureau to carry two names: the OKB

headed by Artem Mikoyan and Mikhail Guryevich.

Mikoyan and Guryevich had both been involved in major programmes before they joined forces on a new VVS fighter requirement in 1938. Mikoyan had worked on the Polikarpov I-153 biplane fighter; his partner had just returned from the highly un-Stalinist atmosphere of Santa Monica, California, where he had been helping Boris Lisunov turn the DC-3 licence into hardware.

The bureau is established

Mikoyan was 34, and Guryevich 46, when the new bureau was formally established in October 1939. Among early recruits to the OKB was a young man named Rostislav Belyakov, who at the time of writing heads the MiG team. The bureau's first fighter prototype flew in April 1940.

The team's first objective was the design of high-performance, high-altitude fighters. Initial results were not impressive. The badly flawed I-200 prototype was rushed into service as the MiG-1, and suffered a catastrophic accident rate. The MiG-3 was an improved version, but entered service just in time for the German invasion. The VVS found itself fighting a low-level, tactical air war, and production of the MiG-3's highly supercharged, high-altitude AM-39 engine was terminated in 1942, bringing to an end wartime production of MiG designs.

The bureau's work on high-altitude fighters continued; the sporadic but potentially dangerous threat from very-high-altitude bombers and reconnaissance aircraft was enough to sustain support for such programmes. A series of successively improved prototypes appeared, incorporating such advanced features as turbosupercharging, cockpit pressurization and laminar-flow aerofoil sections. The last of the series was the excellent I-225, designed for medium-to-high altitude and offering better all-round performance than any contemporary Soviet type. It flew in March 1945; Germany was defeated before it could enter production, and it was superseded by more advanced jet aircraft.

A contemporary of the I-225 deserves mention: the MiG I-250, which may have been the fastest propeller-equipped fighter to enter service. Together with the very similar Su-5, it was developed in great haste to meet the potential threat from German jet aircraft such as the Arado Ar 234 bomber. The Soviet Union's own work on jet engines was lagging far behind Germany's and Britain's; to produce a high-speed interceptor, the MAP developed a unique powerplant coupling a piston engine with a Campini-type jet. Also called an 'accelerator', this resembled a conventional jet without the turbine; instead, the compressor was driven by a shaft from the back of the engine. The auxiliary jet exhausted through a variable rear nozzle.

The I-250 was a notably small aircraft for its power, and used an advanced wing section with slotted flaps. It was claimed to be capable of 513mph (825km/h) in level flight – slightly faster than some early jets. A few I-250s were built, and, designated MiG-13, served with shore-based navy air defence units until 1950.

With fighting in Europe at an end, the wartime East-West alliance died almost as quickly as the pre-war German-Soviet non-aggression pact had done. The effect of the sudden shift in policy on the fortunes of the MiG bureau was immense; in fact, it was to catapult the OKB to the leading position among Soviet fighter design teams, in less than three years. The possibility of an invasion from ruined Europe could be ignored; instead, the threat came from the United States, with its nuclear weapons, a vast fleet of B-29s in being and the intercontinental B-36 under development. The Soviet Union needed jet interceptors, and the MiG OKB, for all its lack of production designs during the war, was pre-eminent in all the necessary technologies: pressure cabins, high-speed aerodynamics, and advanced structures. In April 1946, the MiG bureau flew the first Soviet jet aircraft.

This aircraft, the I-300, was a bulky but basically clean design with two engines

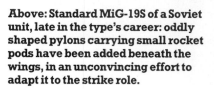

Above: Standard MiG-19S of a Soviet unit, late in the type's career: oddly shaped pylons carrying small rocket pods have been added beneath the wings, in an unconvincing effort to adapt it to the strike role.

Left: A MiG-19PF with Izumrud radar and the inevitable external tanks. Not a large aircraft, the MiG-19 weighs about as much as an A-4 Skyhawk, but with its twin engines it is significantly more powerful.

in the belly, fed by a nose intake. It entered production as the MiG-9. Its aerodynamics were based to some extent on those of the smaller I-250; it carried a heavy armament and had a respectable internal fuel capacity. Its main drawback was an uninspiring thrust/weight ratio, but this was hardly the designers' fault. The Soviet Union's own jet engines were not ready to fly; however, most of the German aero-engine industry had been overrun by Soviet forces, and the entire operation was evacuated to the Soviet Union. (This included many leading designers, who remained there, well treated, until they were permitted to leave in the late 1950s.) Unfortunately, German industry had never produced a

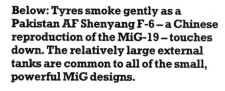

Below: A Bulgarian MiG-19PF undergoing line maintenance. Note the hinged access panels over avionics and systems bays in front of the cockpit, beneath the forward fuselage and over the wing.

Below: Tyres smoke gently as a Pakistan AF Shenyang F-6 – a Chinese reproduction of the MiG-19 – touches down. The relatively large external tanks are common to all of the small, powerful MiG designs.

good turbojet over 2,500lb (1,100kg), thrust, despite its early start, and this limited what early Soviet jets could do.

The breakthrough came in September 1946, when the British Government agreed to provide samples of the 5,000lb (2,720kg) Rolls-Royce Nene engine to the Soviet Union. The Nenes arrived in October, and were promptly and efficiently 'reverse-engineered' by Vladimir Klimov's design team: they were disassembled, all components and tolerances were measured, the materials were analyzed, and the results were translated into new engineering drawings. The first Soviet-built RD-45s were completed early in 1947.

The availability of an engine galvanized an already existing effort to develop a high-performance interceptor, which had been proceeding under Guryevich's leadership while Mikoyan led the urgent effort to get the MiG-9 into service. The MiG team had studied many documents from Germany, and the design which emerged – initially known as Aircraft S – to some extent resembled Dr Kurt Tank's Ta 183, including such features as a swept wing with slight anhedral, a short rear fuselage and a large, highly swept fin carrying the tailplane. As the I-310, it flew at the end of 1947. Tests revealed no problems that could not be tolerated or quickly overcome, and the design was ordered into production in March 1948 as the MiG-15.

Reputation for fighters
The MiG-15 was not merely the best Soviet fighter of its generation; it was the only one to be built in significant numbers, and it established the OKB as the Soviet Union's leading fighter design team. The MiG-15bis, with a more powerful VK-1 engine (the Soviet equivalent of the Rolls-Royce Tay/J48), quickly followed the initial version into production. In Korea, the type proved superior in some respects to the F-86 Sabre, which owed its overall superiority to important features such as its radar gunsight, and benefited from better pilot training and tactics. The MiG-15UTI became the standard Soviet-bloc advanced trainer for decades, while the basic fighter version was built in vast numbers, both in the Soviet Union and in Poland, Czechoslovakia and China.

One of the MiG-15's deficiencies was its inability to exceed Mach 0.92 safely; in fact, the Mach sensor and airbrakes were connected to prevent such a thing from happening. Development of a version without this limitation began in early 1949; the first prototype was flown in January 1950, but was destroyed soon afterwards. The improved SI-2 flew some months later, and production of the new aircraft – the MiG-17 – was authorized in mid-1951.

The MiG-17 was distinguished by a new, more sharply swept wing and tailplane, and a longer and less sharply tapered rear fuselage. Many components, such as the entire forward fuselage, the engine, the armament installation and the landing gear, were similar or identical to those of the MiG-15. The modifications raised the limiting Mach number of the aircraft, but also increased its weight while the thrust remained the same.

The new aircraft did not replace the MiG-15 in production until it was fitted with an augmented VK-1F engine; the result was the MiG-17F, the first reheat-equipped (afterburning) fighter in the Soviet inventory. A radar-equipped version, the MiG-17PF, was developed for the PVO, and was followed by the MiG-17PFU, with four underwing K-5M missiles. MiG-17 production ran to over 6,000 aircraft in the Soviet Union, and the type was also built in Poland, Czechoslovakia and, in very large numbers, in China. Although technically obsolete by the mid-1960s, the type proved a dangerous opponent for US fighters in Vietnam.

Supersonic speed in level flight was the logical next step. It was approached by evolution from the MiG-15 and MiG-17, the first supersonic prototype using the same forward and centre fuselage geometry, mated to a yet longer rear fuselage, a more powerful engine and a new wing and tail of increased sweepback. As was the case with similar developments in the West, it proved more difficult than expected. The mid-set tail of the early prototype aircraft, the I-350, caused flutter problems. The single-engined version was dropped in favour of a parallel development, using two small, very light but respectably powerful AM-5 engines, designed at the Mikulin OKB by Sergei Tumansky. The third prototype in the series, the I-350M, flew

Above: The potential handling problems of the MiG-19's highly swept wing were countered by the use of very large wing fences. One wag suggested that their function was to prevent the airflow from defecting to the tips.

Left: All-round vision hood, two heavy cannon and effective airbrakes made the MiG-19 a fairly effective dogfighter, by the standard of the day.

in September 1953, featuring two engines and a fuselage-mounted tailplane.

The first production aircraft in the series was the MiG-19F, with afterburning AM-5F engines, but the type was barely acceptable for service because of poor handling characteristics. The first effective version was the MiG-19S, with an all-moving slab tail, roll spoilers and other critical changes, which entered service in 1955. Like its immediate predecessor, the MiG-17, the MiG-19 was also delivered with a limited-performance radar (MiG-19PF) and K-5M missiles (MiG-19PM). Some 2,500 MiG-19s were built in the Soviet Union; an even greater number may have been built in China, which reverse-engineered the type after the Sino-Soviet rift of 1960. The

MiG-19 copy, the Shenyang J-6, led to the locally developed JT-6 trainer, and to the considerably modified Q-5 attack fighter; all the Chinese developments have been extensively exported in recent years under the export designations F-6, FT-6 and A-5.

By the mid-1950s, the MiG OKB had achieved every significant 'first' in the development of Soviet jet fighters: first jet to fly, and first in service; first swept-wing fighter in service, and first in combat; first jet fighter with reheat, and first with missile armament. Finally, with the MiG-19, the team had produced not only the first and only workable supersonic fighter in the Soviet Union, but the first in the world. The MiG bureau had come a long way in ten short and eventful years.

MiG-21 'Fishbed'

Small, fast, and austere to a fault, the MiG-21 epitomises the Soviet approach to warplane design and development. The MiG-21 has been in production longer than any other fighter in history, has been built in greater numbers than any other supersonic fighter and has taken part in every air war, bar the South Atlantic, since 1965. Even now, serious studies of re-engined MiG-21s with new sensors and other improvements are being undertaken, because the MiG-21 is such a good answer to the needs of the smaller air force. For an aircraft which Western analysts once dismissed as useless, this is not bad going.

Once the physical and psychological barrier of Mach 1 had been breached, aerospace technology advanced at a gallop. The 1950s saw all previous records for speed and altitude shattered. They were a time of serious work on near-hypersonic aircraft, airborne nuclear power, radical chemical fuels and previously undreamt-of weapons and sensors. It was also the decade in which the Cold War between East and West froze solid.

The Soviet Union's development of nuclear and thermonuclear weapons, and the Korean War of 1950-53, set the international tone for the decade, and there was very little change in the atmosphere from 1950 to 1960. The mood was one of sullen confrontation, and East and West both armed themselves – almost exclusively – for total war.

The 1950s concept of total war was not the same as today's. Nuclear weapons still had to be delivered by subsonic bombers, far more susceptible to interception than today's missiles. The total number of warheads on either side was smaller, because nuclear weapons were difficult and expensive to produce,

and so large that only a handful could be carried on one aircraft. Moreover, the public at large was kept blissfully unaware of the hazards of radioactive fallout. For these reasons, it was felt that non-nuclear combat could still be important, even in the case of an all-out thermonuclear exchange. Another difference between the 1950s and the two subsequent decades was that defence against nuclear attack was considered to be feasible and essential.

Neither the Soviet Union nor the United States, however, could afford to maintain vast land forces while racing to develop new systems for strategic attack and defence. The US had moved to consolidate its alliances in Europe, leading to the establishment of the North Atlantic Treaty Organization in 1949. In 1955 a 'Treaty of Friendship, Mutual Assistance and Cooperation' was signed in Warsaw by the USSR and six other East European states, ostensibly as a defensive response to NATO; in fact, the Warsaw Pact formalized relationships which had existed since the establishment of Communist governments in Eastern Europe in the aftermath of the war. In both cases,

there was a need for conventional weapons to equip these forces, as well as the Soviet and US units that would be based alongside them.

In the USA, the advance of technology had driven the air-defence interceptors and tactical fighters apart by the early 1950s, to the point where the aircraft designed for one mission were incapable of performing the other, even with adaptation. The Soviet Union, however, continued to require all-purpose fighters in the mould of the MiG-15, MiG-17 and MiG-19.

The strategic bomber threat

Several factors influenced Soviet planning for advanced fighters in the early 1950s. One was the rapid expansion of the USAF force of jet bombers. In just four years of production, starting in 1952, the USAF built the staggering total of 2,000 Boeing B-47s, whose Mach 0.9 cruising speed rendered the MiG-15 and MiG-17 impotent, and the MiG-19 of marginal usefulness. The low-time B-50 bombers which the B-47s replaced were converted into tankers; together with the availability of bases in Britain and else-

Above: The small size of the MiG-21F is apparent in this view. The design of the canopy was influenced by that of the Folland Gnat; it formed a blast shield to protect the pilot in the event of ejection.

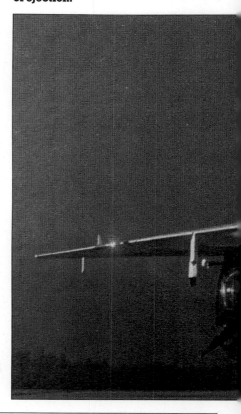

Below: Czech-built MiG-21Fs, produced at the Aero factory near Prague and designated S-107, can be distinguished from otherwise similar Soviet-built machines by the lack of a glazed rear section to the canopy.

Bottom: The Tumansky R-11 was a remarkable engine. The two-spool powerplant has a high thrust/weight ratio, and contains only 3,500 parts, fewer than the much smaller J85, thanks to good basic design.

Below: A pristine S-107 (MiG-21F). Note that the port gun has been removed, making way for additional electronics. The combined pitot boom and yaw/pitch sensors is a standard piece of equipment.

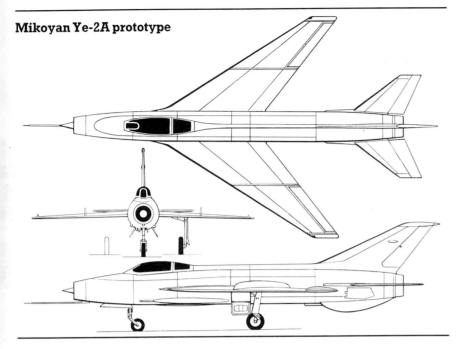

Mikoyan Ye-2A prototype

Above: The aerodynamic configuration of the Ye-2A was based on a thin-winged MiG-19. The less conventional delta-winged Ye-5, with a lower empty weight, proved to have better performance in all respects.

Below: Through ingenious design, it proved possible to fit a radar in the already tightly packed airframe, creating the MiG-21PF. Note the oversize, low-pressure tyres common to all MiG-21s.

Above: a MiG-21F of the DDR Luftstreitkrafte slows down for the camera, displaying its three small ventral airbrakes. The aircraft in the background is a later model, with a broader fin and relocated brake chute.

where, this made the B-47's relatively short range very much less important. B-47 attacks could be expected from almost any direction. Meanwhile, the intercontinental B-52 was well advanced in development. As well as adding a truly global dimension to the jet bomber threat, it would carry more extensive countermeasures than the B-47 and would cruise at higher altitudes.

Combat experience in Korea was also important. While the kill/loss ratio had been heavily in favour of the USAF (probably about 4:1, rather than the 10:1 claimed at the time) there was little dispute that the basic design of the MiG-15 had proved sound. A few small but significant items of equipment, and much better training and experience, had decided many engagements. In terms of performance and firepower, the MiG-15 had held its own against the much larger F-86. Korea also demonstrated that tactical air warfare could still come down to a close-range, turning engagement, and that absolute performance, including speed, acceleration and rate-of-climb, was important; an aircraft with the advantage in performance gave its pilot

the initiative in starting or ending an engagement.

Basic Soviet military doctrine, however, introduced a complication into the conception of any new Soviet fighter: numerical superiority was vital. Western Mach 2 fighters were, without exception, more complex and more expensive than their subsonic and transonic predecessors. There were fewer of them, and they needed more maintenance. Such a development would have been unacceptable to the Soviet front commander, who then as now considered numbers first and technical quality second. Resolving the dilemma by increasing the resources devoted to fighter production was out of the question; bomber production took absolute priority, and it would be years before the Soviet strategic strike force attained parity with Strategic Air Command.

The requirement

The solution was to issue a requirement in late 1953, calling for a fighter with Mach 2 speed, and a service ceiling close to 66,000ft (20,000m) – both figures based on what was necessary to engage a B-52 – but demanding that the aircraft be little bigger than a MiG-17, and actually smaller than a MiG-19. Moreover, the aircraft had to carry a range-only radar, air-to-air missiles and a pair of heavy cannon, and it had to possess conventional flying characteristics, good manoeuvrability and reasonable field performance.

By the standards of the time this was a very stiff requirement indeed. The small size was the root of most of the problems it posed. Many of the components of the aircraft were basically fixed in size and weight; the pilot, seat and cockpit enclosure, the radar and radio equipment, the guns and the missiles were examples. They tended to make a fixed contribution to the weight and drag of the aircraft, and some of them imposed other constraints, such as the cockpit, which required a minimum cross-section forward of the wing. The main reason why Western designs had grown in weight and size was to reduce the weight and drag of these fixed items as a proportion of the total-aircraft figures.

The call for high supersonic speed compounded the difficulties. The aircraft was to be small, its internal fuel capacity would not be great, and it accordingly

Left: Details apparent on this S-107 include the ogival centrebody and the large vertical wheel wells. Note the large Fowler flaps, fully extended for take-off. The aircraft may be taking off on dry thrust in order to conserve its limited supply of fuel.

Mikoyan SM-12PM

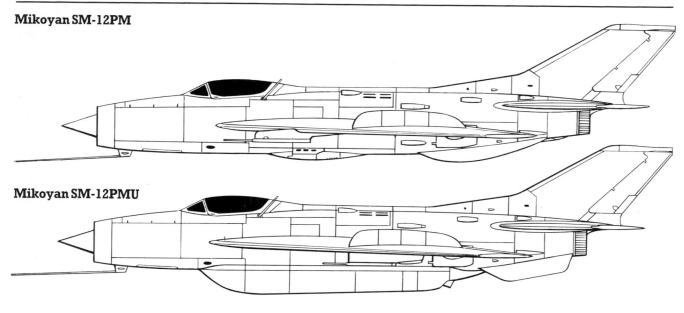

Mikoyan SM-12PMU

cated handling. Under TsAGI control, the MiG trademarks appeared on everything from cruise missiles to the Mya-4 heavy bomber.

Another feature which was probably assumed from the start was the inlet design. All previous Soviet fighters and prototypes had featured nose intakes, so the adoption of any other configuration would have meant a simultaneous move into a new internal geometry and a new speed range. The design has advantages of its own: it mandates long, gradually curved ducts, which tend to generate few surprises; the inlet itself is free from problems caused by wakes and vortices from the airframe or gun gas ingestion; and the air enters the inlet as it has to enter the engine, equally distributed in a circular pattern. The two main drawbacks are that such a layout takes up a large volume in the forward fuselage, and makes it almost impossible to install an engine with greater mass flow at a later date.

Above: The more advanced inlet and radar nose configuration of the MiG-21PF was tested on two highly modified MiG-19s with broad-chord vertical fins. The SM-12PMU added a large ventral rocket pack.

Right: The MiG-21PFM featured plain, blown flaps. These were less efficient on take-off than the original Fowler flaps, so provision was made for the execution of flapless, rocket-assisted short take-offs.

could not afford an oversized engine. An efficient supersonic configuration was vital. The Area Rule called for a smooth, and not excessive, variation in cross-sectional area from nose to tail, and the need to reduce wave drag meant that the fuselage must be as slender as possible. Neither was readily compatible with a light, efficiently packed airframe of small overall dimensions.

The new fighter would be single-engined – there is no evidence that any other layout was considered. The development of the Tumansky RD-9 had built up experience in small, light, powerful turbojets to the point where the design of a slightly larger engine would not present too many problems, and a

single-engined aircraft would have a more slender, lighter rear fuselage than a twin of the same size.

The overall layout of the aircraft was strongly influenced by the aerodynamicists at the MAP's Central Aero-Hydrodynamics Institute (TsAGI). At that time TsAGI's influence was at its zenith, and its technical authority was such that its recommendations were almost read as law. However, TsAGI itself was strongly influenced by the success of the earlier MiG fighters, whose mid-set wings and circular-section fuselages may have been less than ideal from the systems-packaging standpoint, but were aerodynamically straightforward and contributed to low drag and uncompli-

Planforms for supersonic flight were many and various in the early 1950s. Thin, moderately swept wings, tailless deltas, ultra-thin straight wings and other layouts were all being tried, with varying degrees of success, but most of them were ruled out for the new Soviet fighter by the terms of the requirement. Medium sweep angles were limited to about Mach 1.5 with contemporary powerplant technology; tailless deltas and F-104-type thin wings would not have achieved the necessary runway performance with existing technology.

Alternative solutions

TsAGI proposed two solutions. One was to modify the MiG-19 wing for a higher Mach number; the other was a new layout, combining a sharply swept delta wing with a tailplane. The basic delta had been flown in 1949, on the Convair XF-92A prototype, and despite its outlandish appearance it had shown itself to be free of vices or surprises. Its drag was little higher than that of a swept wing, but it offered much more volume, had more area for the same weight, and was inherently stiff. Its main disadvantage was that it replaced the normal tailplane; at low speed, instead of flaps lifting the aircraft, the delta wing had up-elevon weighing it down. The delta also generated its maximum lift at very high angles of attack, which were impractical for conventional aircraft. Finally, the fact that the relatively short trailing edge had to provide all the pitch and roll forces for the aircraft, with a short moment arm, made the delta less manoeuvrable than a conventional aircraft.

Adding a conventional tail relieved many of the problems and produced a layout with inherently good stability and

handling. In particular, the delta's ability to maintain stable airflow up to high angles of attack – as a result of vortices shed by its sharply swept leading edge – was retained. This was important for a fighter, because it meant that the ailerons remained effective at virtually all times, and the pilot could pull very hard manoeuvres without worrying about losing lateral control.

The only serious limitation of the layout was that its short span, thin section and high sweep militated against high wing loadings. Even with large and effective flaps, the TsAGI-type tailed delta would not be a champion weight-lifter, and growth potential would be limited. (The West's only tailed delta, the A-4 Skyhawk, carries heavy external loads, but has a thicker, slatted wing.) However, future growth beyond the scope of the requirement was not something which the Soviet system considered important.

In early 1954, the MAP directed the MiG bureau to build prototypes of the small supersonic fighter with both swept and delta wings. A near-parallel programme, also started in 1954, called for swept-wing and delta-wing prototypes of very similar configuration, but larger. Clearly, MAP was concerned that the MiG-17 sized aircraft might not meet all the requirements, particularly the evolving needs of the PVO.

The challenge facing the MiG bureau was to fit all the components of an advanced fighter aircraft into the close confines of the TsAGI configuration. This was done with considerable ingenuity, and work on the new prototypes – all designated with the Soviet letter written as E, but pronounced Ye - forged ahead. To a Western eye, the internal layout of the new aircraft would have seemed ran-

Above: The introduction of the Mach 2, radar-equipped MiG-21PF was a major step forward for the non-Soviet Warsaw Pact forces. This example is a member of a single regiment of MiG-21PFs supplied to Romania.

Below: Each Soviet fighter regiment contains two or three two-seaters for conversion training. In this scene at a SovAF base, a MiG-21U 'Mongol-A' taxies out for a training mission, with an Su-7 following it.

Below: MiG-21FL was the designation of this subtype, built by HAL at Nasik. It was basically similar to a late-production MiG-21PF, but had an export-model radar and a more powerful version of the R-11 engine.

Below: The second-generation MiG-21s were the first to have radar, a major omission from the original. Note that the HAL aircraft, built later than the Soviet types, has a GP-9 gun pack housing a twin-barrel GSh-23.

Second-generation MiG-21s

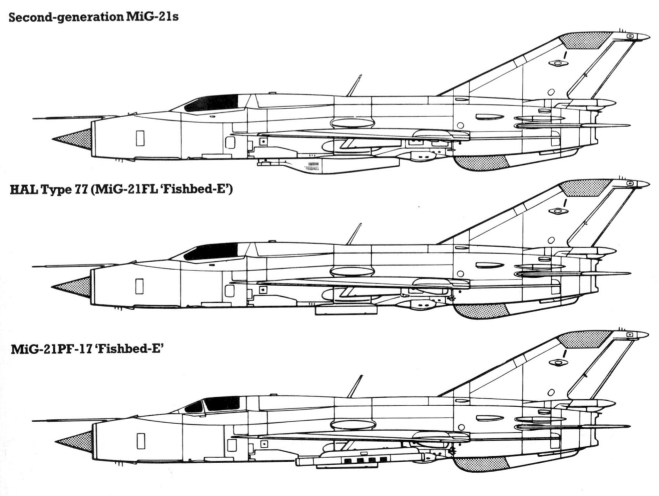

HAL Type 77 (MiG-21FL 'Fishbed-E')

MiG-21PF-17 'Fishbed-E'

MiG-21PFM 'Fishbed-F'

dom and disorganized, and the exterior appearance untidy. However, the nature of the design becomes much clearer when the packaging problem is considered.

The core of the design was a new engine from the Tumansky bureau, the R-11. There has been some controversy over whether this engine was a two-shaft design. Its thrust and diameter, however, suggest a pressure ratio in the region of 10:1-12:1. In the West, such pressures have been combined with acceptable handling by two means: the use of a two-spool layout, the extensive use of variable stators or the use of a large number of compressor stages. The R-11 emerged as a two-spool engine, the first Soviet engine to feature such a layout. For its day (it was probably first run in prototype form in 1953), the R-11's design thrust/weight ratio of 5:1 was quite ambitious; it was achieved partly by straightforward, economical design – the engine was astoundingly simple, with a total of only 3,500 different parts – and partly by deliberately sacrificing durability.

The latter aspect is important. In Soviet terms, reliability is distinct from durability. Reliability directly affects the performance of the weapon in combat, and there is nothing to be done if a critical failure occurs in action. Absolute reliability is the goal. Durability, on the other hand, is something which is only vital to a certain degree. In Western terms, an engine which must be returned to a large maintenance depot, stripped, disassembled and checked and repaired where necessary every 250 hours is an abomination. In the Soviet Union, a time between overhauls (TBO) of 250-300hr is not uncommon, and the reasoning behind this fact is interesting.

Maintenance logistics

As noted in the previous chapter, the combat units are not expected to worry about fixing their aircraft and engines, beyond the most elementary maintenance (which is made as easy as possible, with plenty of small, quick-opening panels for routine inspections). Instead, they run them for their allotted lifetimes and exchange them for newly overhauled equipment, fresh from the maintenance depot. The conservative TBOs mean that unscheduled removals are rare, and the engines need little inspection in service. The logistics system is geared to handle all the overhaul work and the traffic in repaired components, and generally works smoothly because nearly all the work is scheduled.

In fact, the TBO requirement is set by the needs of the Front commander. He knows that his logistic system will not work smoothly in wartime; essentially, he needs enough time on the weapons he has available to fight the war. Assuming that, at any given time, his fighter engines will have an average of half their TBO left, the target TBO is twice as many hours as the fighter is expected to fly in the course of the main offensive.

In the case of engines, the short TBOs make it possible to achieve higher thrust/weight ratio and better fuel consumption. Both these figures improve with increasing engine pressure ratio, but this also means higher temperatures in the engine. Much of the advanced and expensive technology in Western engines is devoted to achieving long life with high temperatures; Soviet metallurgy is not quite as advanced as that of the West, but engine performance is closely comparable because long TBOs are not required.

Given the size of the R-11, the fuselage design of the MiG prototypes was built up around the engine and its inlet trunk, which was split vertically just behind the inlet lip and merged just ahead of the

engine. Structurally, it was basically similar to the earlier MiGs. The wings were separate – being removable for transport and repair, as MAP requires – and attached by lugs and bolts to high-strength forged steel ring-bulkheads with stainless-steel fittings. These bulkheads were the heart of the aircraft. The inlet ducts, and the main fuel tanks between them, fitted inside the ring. The rear fuselage bolted to the rearmost bulkhead, and the forward fuselage – designed around the pilot's seat, the electronics bay and the inlets – was attached to the front. The nosewheel bay served a dual purpose, providing access to the lower electronics bay; a single bonnet-like panel ahead of the windscreen hinged forward to give access to the upper part of the bay.

Internally, the design reflected the need for minimum cross-section, with a number of notable features. In the nose, a single aluminium panel on each side extended from just behind the inlet to the leading-edge wing root, and from the cockpit sill to the lower part of the fuselage; it formed both the side of the fuselage and the outer wall of the inlet duct. Neither of the small, thin-section wings

Above: A Yugoslav Air Force MiG-21PFM, fresh from its regular overhaul. Soviet support practice relies on frequent major overhauls, conducted at factory-type rates.

Below: Two Soviet MiG-21PFMs, ready to roll on a night intercept training mission. With reheat used for take-off, the operational radius will not be substantial.

Right: The number of early-production MiG-21PFs, codenamed 'Fishbed-D', with the same narrow-chord fin as the MiG-21F, was not large. This example was assigned to a display team, possibly formed by the Moscow Air Defence District.

Right: The third-generation MiG-21, represented by this Yugoslav MF, was a major advance. The mix of air-to-air and air-to-surface weaponry shown on this aircraft was theoretically possible, if unusual. The outboard pylons were plumbed for fuel tanks.

Left: A well-used early-model MiG-21PF of the Polish Air Force. The prominence of the rivets is due to the use of steel rivets, which are prone to surface corrosion.

would accommodate the landing gear without the use of small high-pressure tyres, but these would have been operationally unacceptable because of the requirement to operate from quickly prepared strips or cleared tundra. A fuselage-mounted gear, however, would have had too narrow a track. The answer was an ingenious inward-retracting gear, in which the wheels were attached to the legs by a complex but sturdy mechanical linkage. As the legs folded into the wing, the wheels remained in a near-vertical position and retracted into the fuselage sides between the main bulkheads.

New design trademark

Because the wheels were a little too large for the space available, the designers added small bulges in the fuselage and gear doors above and below the wheel wells. This proved to be the start of a design trademark. Soviet designers, unlike their Western counterparts, never seem too afraid of adding small bulges in the skin to ease a problem of internal design, to add strength or simplify construction, or to avoid having to enlarge the overall cross-section. They do nothing for the looks of the aircraft, but cause very little extra drag, especially toward the rear, where the airflow over the skin is already broken up.

The design of the stabilizer also deserves special note. The aim was the slimmest possible rear fuselage, but the aerodynamic configuration called for an all-moving stabilizer at mid-height, in line with the wings. On the MiG-19 the stabilizer was set at the top of the fuselage, and the two halves were deeply rooted in the structure; that would not be possible with the new aircraft, because the jetpipe was in the way. Both stabilizers would have to transmit their loads separately into the side of the fuselage.

The solution was to adopt the same geometry as used for the MiG-19. The trunnions on which the tail pivoted were angled in line with the sweepback at half-chord. In Western designs, the trunnions are usually at 90° to the fuselage; the MiG method carries the loads into the fuselage further forward, so that the main load-bearing structure can be shortened. The tailplanes were linked by bellcranks and rods (one bellcrank accounts for another pimple on each

Above: A mixed Polish Air Force formation containing three MiG-21PFMs and (furthest from camera) an early MiG-21PF. Operationally, the aircraft were interchangeable.

Below: An unusual interim (or, possibly, updated) MiG-21PF with the early narrow-chord fin, later braking-chute arrangement and provision for rocket-assisted take-off.

side) to the single actuator and the artificial-feel system, in the leading edge of the fin. This layout also placed the stabilizer and rudder actuators close to the engine ancillaries, reducing the length of the hydraulic system.

That much was common to the two different versions. The swept wing was based on the MiG-19 structural design, with two spars and ribs at right angles to the leading edge. The delta featured a full-span swept main spar, supported by two unswept boxes forming another structural box. Large, area-increasing Fowler flaps were fitted to the trailing edge of the delta wing.

The first in the series to fly was the swept-wing Ye-50, in late 1955. The R-11 was not ready, so the Ye-50 was fitted with a single RD-9 (the MiG-19 engine) and a rocket engine in the tail. It attained Mach 2.3, and while the mixed-power fighter was never adopted for service use, the Ye-50 demonstrated that the swept wing was structurally and aerodynamically sound. The definitive R-11-powered prototypes – the swept-wing Ye-2A and the delta Ye-5 - flew in May and June 1956 respectively, and made the short flight from GAZ 155 to Tushino for the Aviation Day flypast.

This brief appearance had an interesting sequel. Firstly, Western intelligence failed to appreciate the small size of the MiG fighters, believing them to be about the same size as the Sukhoi types which made their debut at the same time. Secondly, the Western analysts became convinced that the Ye-2A, codenamed 'Faceplate', had entered production, while the delta-winged Ye-5 'Fishbed' had been abandoned. In mitigation, it should be pointed out that the simultaneous fielding of two Sukhoi fighters with very similar layouts confused the situation. However, the misconceptions concerning the MiG fighters were to endure for half a decade.

In fact, it was the Ye-5 that was selected as the basis for the production aircraft, mainly because its thicker wing gave it more internal fuel capacity, at the end of 1956. Neither type had shown any serious aerodynamic vices; the problems that were encountered affected the Ye-2A and Ye-5 equally. The two most serious of these concerned engine/inlet matching and the flight control system.

Problems with the first true supersonic inlet in the Soviet Union were not surprising. The design was classically simple, a derivative of the conventional blunt-lipped circular inlet used on earlier MiGs; that design worked well up to Mach 1.4, but shock-waves formed from the lip generated an increasing amount of drag at higher speeds. The Ye-2A/Ye-50 inlet had a sharp lip, and a pointed central cone. The aerodynamic function of the inlet cone was to form a shock wave – the primary shock – ahead of the inlet aperture, decelerating the air (relative to the aircraft) before it entered the inlet. This type of inlet is simple, and works well under test conditions; the problem with the original Ye-2A/Ye-50 inlet was that it had no variable geometry whatsoever, and could not accommodate the full range of speeds and altitudes of which the aircraft was capable.

Adjustable inlet

The solution was an adjustable three-position centre-body, automatically controlled according to airspeed, which allowed the airflow to be matched to the flight conditions and the needs of the engine. Also, the area of the basic inlet was reduced to avoid compressor stalls, while to aid in starting, relighting and low-speed flight, small auxiliary suck-in doors were added just below the wing leading edge. A final addition was a spill door on each side of the nose, to relieve

Above: Another unusual variant: an early-model MiG-21PFMA, first of the third generation, delivered to Czechoslovakia before the GSh-23 internal gun was available. The anti-ingestion strakes are also absent.

Below: A Soviet pilot poses for the camera with his MiG-21MF. The boom-mounted pitch and yaw sensors, absent from the second-generation types and the PFMA, made a comeback on this and later versions.

Mikoyan MiG-21MF 'Fishbed-J' cutaway

1 Pitot-static boom
2 Pitch vanes
3 Yaw vanes
4 Conical three-position intake centrebody
5 'Spin Scan' search-and-track radar antenna
6 Boundary layer slot
7 Engine air intake
8 Radar ('Spin Scan')
9 Lower boundary layer exit
10 Antennas
11 Nosewheel doors
12 Nosewheel leg and shock absorbers
13 Castoring nosewheel
14 Anti-shimmy damper
15 Avionics bay access
16 Attitude sensor
17 Nosewheel well
18 Spill door
19 Nosewheel retraction pivot
20 Bifurcated intake trunking
21 Avionics bay
22 Electronics equipment
23 Intake trunking
24 Upper boundary layer exit
25 Dynamic pressure probe for q-feel
26 Semi-elliptical armour-glass windscreen
27 Gunsight mounting
28 Fixed quarterlight
29 Radar scope
30 Control column (with tailplane trim switch and two firing buttons)
31 Rudder pedals
32 Underfloor control runs
33 KM-1 two-position zero-level ejection seat
34 Port instrument console

35 Undercarriage handle
36 Seat harness
37 Canopy release/lock
38 Starboard wall switch panel
39 Rear-view mirror fairing
40 Starboard-hinged canopy
41 Ejection seat headrest
42 Avionics bay
43 Control rods
44 Air conditioning plant
45 Suction relief door
46 Intake trunking
47 Wingroot attachment fairing
48 Wing/fuselage spar-lug attachment points (four)
49 Fuselage ring frames
50 Intermediary frames
51 Main fuselage fuel tank
52 RSIU radio bay
53 Auxiliary intake
54 Leading edge integral fuel tank
55 Starboard outer weapons pylon
56 Outboard wing construction
57 Starboard navigation light
58 Leading edge suppressed antenna
59 Wing fence
60 Aileron control jack
61 Starboard aileron
62 Flap actuator fairing
63 Starboard blown flap
64 Multi-spar wing structure
65 Main integral wing fuel tank

66 Undercarriage mounting/pivot point
67 Starboard main wheel leg
68 Auxiliaries compartment
69 Fuselage fuel tanks Nos 2 and 3
70 Mainwheel well external fairing
71 Mainwheel (retracted)
72 Trunking contours
73 Control rods in dorsal spine
74 Compressor face
75 Oil tank
76 Avionics pack
77 Engine accessories
78 Tumansky R-13 turbojet (rated at 14,550lb/6,600kg with full reheat)
79 Fuselage break/transport joint
80 Intake
81 Tail surface control linkage
82 Artificial feel unit
83 Tailplane jack
84 Hydraulic accumulator
85 Tailplane trim motor
86 Tailfin spar attachment plate
87 Rudder jack
88 Rudder control linkage
89 Tailfin structure
90 Leading edge panel
91 Radio cable access
92 Magnetic detector
93 Tailfin mainspar

excessive pressure in the inlet. Meanwhile, a programme of research into more efficient Mach 2 inlet configurations got under way, using modified MiG-19s.

The control problem was essentially one of systems design. In pursuit of light weight and efficiency, the MiG OKB had provided only a single hydraulic system, with manual back-up for the rudder and ailerons and a standby electrical system for the stabilizer. The first pre-production prototype, the Ye-6, was lost after the engine stalled, and the standby stabilizer control proved inadequate; after that, the system was redesigned around dual hydraulics. The modified aircraft was cleared for production in 1957, as the MiG-21, and deliveries started in the following year.

The initial version, known to NATO as 'Fishbed-A', was not built in large numbers. The flight control system still needed development, handling characteristics still had to be refined, and the engine was not only short of thrust but its TBO of 100 hours was unacceptable even by Soviet standards. However, the initial MiG-21 incorporated most of the features

of the production aircraft, including armament and operational systems.

The main weapon was the K-13A air-to-air missile, known to NATO as AA-2 'Atoll' and very similar to the US Sidewinder. It has often been suggested that the K-13A was copied from one of the US weapons which had been fired from a Chinese Nationalist Air Force F-86 over Quemoy, had struck its target – a Chinese MiG-15 – but had failed to explode, due to simultaneous failures of its proximity fuze, impact fuze and self-destruct system. But this story has never been confirmed, and the resemblance may be one of flattery rather than imitation; most of the world's other missiles in this class bear a strong resemblance to the Sidewinder. Like the early Sidewinder, the original K-13A was a pursuit-course weapon – its IR homing head needed an intense source of radiation, such as the hot metal at the rear of the

Right: Simple, proven construction methods are used in the MiG-21. Note also how components that do not fit the fuselage shape are accommodated in fairings and conduits.

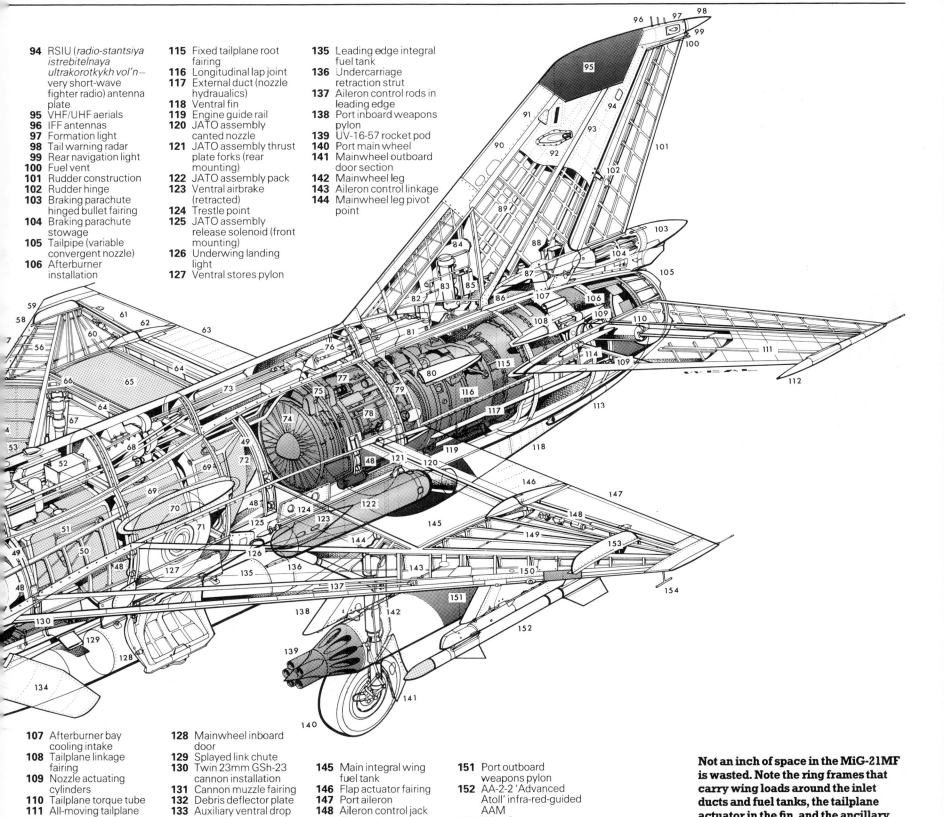

94 RSIU (radio-stantsiya istrebitelnaya istrebitelnaya ultrakorotkykh vol'n– very short-wave fighter radio) antenna plate
95 VHF/UHF aerials
96 IFF antennas
97 Formation light
98 Tail warning radar
99 Rear navigation light
100 Fuel vent
101 Rudder construction
102 Rudder hinge
103 Braking parachute hinged bullet fairing
104 Braking parachute stowage
105 Tailpipe (variable convergent nozzle)
106 Afterburner installation

115 Fixed tailplane root fairing
116 Longitudinal lap joint
117 External duct (nozzle hydraulics)
118 Ventral fin
119 Engine guide rail
120 JATO assembly canted nozzle
121 JATO assembly thrust plate forks (rear mounting)
122 JATO assembly pack
123 Ventral airbrake (retracted)
124 Trestle point
125 JATO assembly release solenoid (front mounting)
126 Underwing landing light
127 Ventral stores pylon

135 Leading edge integral fuel tank
136 Undercarriage retraction strut
137 Aileron control rods in leading edge
138 Port inboard weapons pylon
139 UV-16-57 rocket pod
140 Port main wheel
141 Mainwheel outboard door section
142 Mainwheel leg
143 Aileron control linkage
144 Mainwheel leg pivot point

107 Afterburner bay cooling intake
108 Tailplane linkage fairing
109 Nozzle actuating cylinders
110 Tailplane torque tube
111 All-moving tailplane
112 Anti-flutter weight
113 Intake
114 Afterburner mounting

128 Mainwheel inboard door
129 Splayed link chute
130 Twin 23mm GSh-23 cannon installation
131 Cannon muzzle fairing
132 Debris deflector plate
133 Auxiliary ventral drop tank
134 Port forward air brake (extended)

145 Main integral wing fuel tank
146 Flap actuator fairing
147 Port aileron
148 Aileron control jack
149 Outboard wing construction
150 Port navigation light

151 Port outboard weapons pylon
152 AA-2-2 'Advanced Atoll' infra-red-guided AAM
153 Wing fence
154 Radio altimeter antenna

Not an inch of space in the MiG-21MF is wasted. Note the ring frames that carry wing loads around the inlet ducts and fuel tanks, the tailplane actuator in the fin, and the ancillary equipment moved into the dorsal spine to make room elsewhere.

target's engine, in order to guide correctly.

Faired into the lower fuselage of the MiG-21 were two Nudelman-Rikhter NR-30 cannon, of the type originally used on later production MiG-19s. A revolver cannon of the same general type as the British Aden, French Defa and US M-39, the NR-30 was a powerful weapon with a 14.4oz (410g) projectile, a 2,550ft/sec (780m/sec) muzzle velocity and a rate of fire between 850 and 1,000 rounds per minute. The projectile size, larger even than that of the A-10's fearsome GAU-8/A, is particularly notable.

The weapons were aimed with a simple gyroscopic gunsight, with range information provided by the small radar in the nose cone. The rest of the cockpit was equally simple. Beacon receivers were provided for navigation, but the main emphasis was on ground-to-air links through which the fighter could be vectored to its target. The ejection seat was a specially developed lightweight design, and was linked to the unusual one-piece, forward-hinged canopy; the hood separated from the aircraft with the seat, forming a screen against wind blast.

The first full-scale production version appeared in late 1959. The main change to the MiG-21F was the switch to an uprated engine, the R-11F, with about 10 per cent more power. A number of other significant changes, however, were incorporated in the early stages of production, including a broader-chord fin for improved stability at high Mach numbers. Most MiG-21Fs possessed only one gun, the port NR-30 being removed. It is quite possible that the space was needed for datalink equipment, or for another system displaced by the introduction of the new VHF device.

Airbrake location

Another change during MiG-21F production was the incorporation of two extra airbrakes beneath the fuselage, level with the leading edge, augmenting the original small airbrake ahead of the ventral fin. Three separate airbrakes for a small fighter may seem a lot, but, it seems that one of the requirements common to all Soviet combat aircraft is that extending the airbrakes must not disturb the aircraft in pitch. Neither are brakes allowed to displace the central pylon. The result is that there are few good locations for a single large airbrake, and Soviet fighters tend to have two or more oddly positioned airbrake panels.

The MiG-21F was found to have solved most of the problems of the original MiG-21, and went into large-scale production at Gorkii. The type was also built in

Below: The spartan cockpit of a MiG-21MF. Note the robust ejection handles and the reliable, low-maintenance toggle switches, protected by metal rings from inadvertent operation.

Czechoslovakia, at the Aero plant near Prague; the Czech-built aircraft were distinguished by the absence of rear-vision panels behind their canopies. In April 1963, the first batch of ten MiG-21Fs arrived in Finland, and the Western myth of the 30,000lb (13,600kg) MiG-21 was finally exploded.

In addition, a number of MiG-21Fs were supplied to China in early 1960, before the rapid deterioration of Sino-Soviet relations which started later in that year. All technical assistance had been cut off by the end of 1960, but the MiG-21s, their engines and their missiles were rapidly dissected and reverse-engineered at the Xian State Aircraft Factory. The first Chinese-built aircraft, designated Xian J-7, was flown in December 1964; the R-11F engine was copied at Shenyang as the WP-7B. In the late 1960s, production was suspended, but output resumed following the political changes of the late 1970s.

Recent J-7s, such as the 80 aircraft delivered to Egypt from 1982 onward, incorporate a number of changes, including a conventional rearward-hinged canopy with a separate three-piece windshield, and a small radar warning receiver in a bullet at the base of the rudder. Other J-7s have reportedly been assembled in Egypt and passed on to Iraq.

The MiG-21F corresponded very closely to the 1953 specification; the

Right: The multi-role MiG-21MF had a less obtrusive radar display than the pure interceptor versions. The prominent master caution panel, above and to the right of the radar scope, is also noteworthy.

Above: Head locked firmly into the radar hood, and ears cocked for GCI instructions, were standard procedure for a successful interception in this Polish MiG-21PFM. The small optical sight was for back-up use only.

problem was that the specification itself did not realistically reflect operational needs. By the time the aircraft entered service, it was realised that the limitations of the unaided human eye made a search-and-track radar not merely a desirable option for a high-altitude supersonic interceptor, but a complete necessity unless ground control was extremely tight and accurate. By the time the MiG-21F entered service, design and testing of the radar-equipped second-generation MiG-21 was well under way.

The chosen radar was the R1L, known to NATO as 'Spin Scan' and providing some 100kW of power in I-band, and taking its name from its spiral scanning pattern. Originally designed for the much larger Su-9 'Fishpot-A' interceptor,

the R1L represented a substantial item of equipment for a fighter as small as the MiG-21, and incorporating it without loss of performance was a challenge.

The response to the challenge was to develop a new forward fuselage, probably incorporating many of the lessons learned in the difficult development of the original MiG-21 inlet. A very similar inlet was tested on a modified MiG-19, the SM-12PM, in 1957-58. The new nose was almost untapered, and the inlet was greatly increased in diameter. The capture area was unchanged, being dictated by the engine mass flow; the central cone could therefore be large enough to house the radar antenna. The fact that the cone was larger in relation to the inlet also improved its aerodynamic efficiency, particularly at high speed. The cone slid forward between Mach 1 and Mach 1.2, so as to spill the primary shock past the inlet.

Radar cooling

Another new feature was a narrow annular slot girdling the cone, directly behind the radome. This bled the turbulent boundary layer off the surface of the cone, further improving efficiency. The airflow through the slot was used to cool the radar electronics, mounted in a single pack behind the antenna, before being exhausted through vents above and below the nose. However, cooling airflow was cut off at speeds above Mach 1.2, as the cone slid forward.

Installation of the radar displaced the systems which had previously been fitted ahead of the cockpit, and in order to add internal volume, the designers exploited their understanding of the Area Rule. In place of the minimal dorsal spine, which on the MiG-21F covered the control runs, the OKB extended the top and sill lines of the canopy further aft, providing space for extra equipment. The result was to smooth out the variation of cross-section over the length of the aircraft, reducing drag at Mach 1.2 by 20 per cent and causing no increase in drag at higher speeds, though it did diminish rearward visibility from the cockpit.

The recontoured fuselage was tested on a prototype aircraft, designated Ye-66A, which was also fitted with a belly pack containing a 6,500lb (3,000kg) thrust U-2 liquid-fuel rocket engine and

MiG-21 stores options

1 AA-2-2 'Advanced Atoll' radar-guided air-to-air missile (compatible with 'Jay Bird' radar)
2 UB-16-57 rocket pod
3 57mm rockets
4 500kg general-purpose bomb (a total of 48 types of free-fall bomb, including nuclear, napalm, chemical and fuel-air explosive types, are qualified for use on the MiG-21)
5 108lmp gal (490lit) drop tank; 176lmp gal (800lit) and 286lmp gal (1,300lit) tanks also available
6 GP-9 pack (GSh-23 gun and ammunition)
7 23mm ammunition (normal load 200rds)
8 Reconnaissance pod with forward plus three lateral oblique cameras, IR linescan printer and ECM chaff dispenser
9 AA-8 'Aphid' IR-homing air-to-air missile
10 AA-2 'Atoll' IR-homing air-to-air missile
11 ECM jammer pod

MiG-21 weapons provision and avionics

1 GSh-23 cannon with 200rds ammunition
2 Centreline pylon, capacity 500kg (1,100lb)
3 Inboard wing pylon, capacity 250kg (550lb)
4 Outboard wing pylon
5 'Spin Scan' radar
6 'Odd Rods' IFF antennas
7 Main avionics bay
8 HF notch antenna, ILS
9 Radar altimeter
10 VHF/UHF antenna
11 Radar warning receiver
12 VHF communications and data link antenna

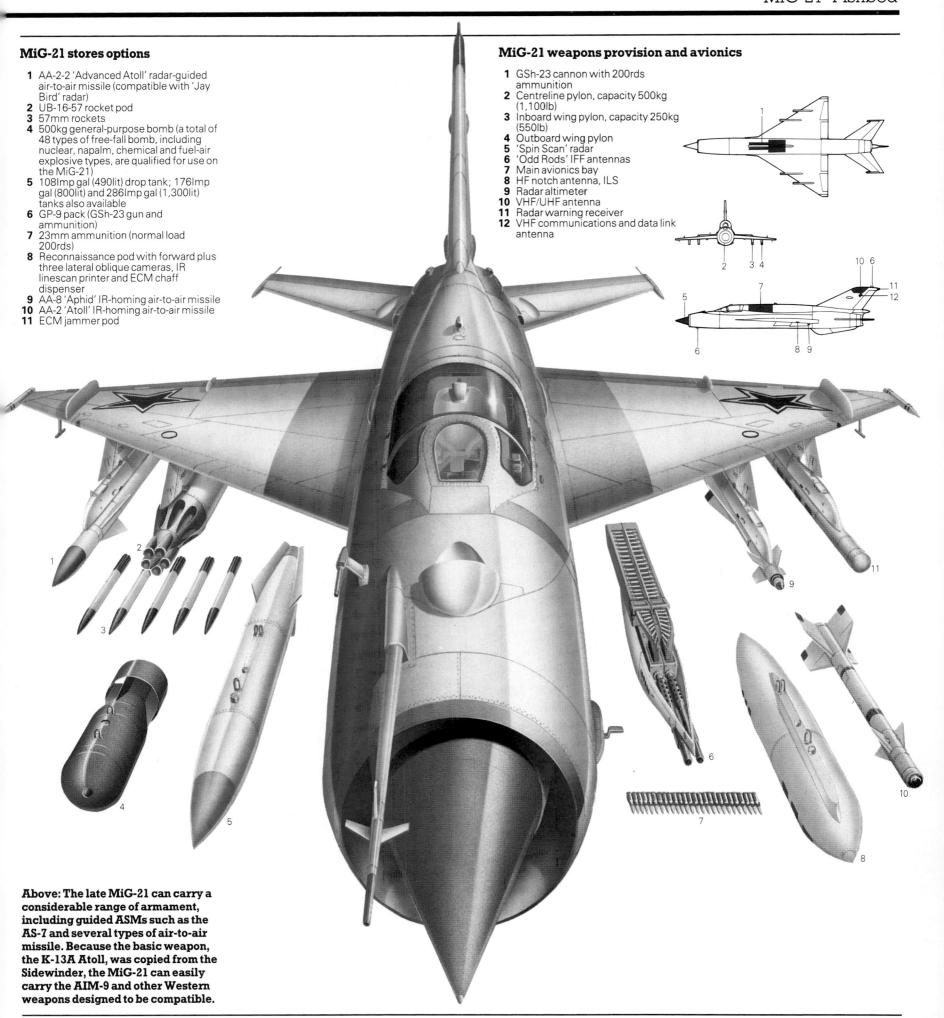

Above: The late MiG-21 can carry a considerable range of armament, including guided ASMs such as the AS-7 and several types of air-to-air missile. Because the basic weapon, the K-13A Atoll, was copied from the Sidewinder, the MiG-21 can easily carry the AIM-9 and other Western weapons designed to be compatible.

Left: The unguided rocket has been a favourite Soviet weapon since the 1940s, providing great firepower and reasonable accuracy without sophisticated aiming systems. This is a UB-16 pod (16 S-5 57mm rockets).

its propellant tank. There is no sign that this layout was being considered for production, but it was used to probe the speed and height limits of the design and set an official world altitude record of 113,891ft (34,714m) on April 28, 1961.

The new version – which flew around 1959, as the Ye-7 – also dispensed with the remaining gun and the corresponding bulges, simplifying the design of the forward airbrakes. Despite the removal of the guns, it was heavier than the MiG-

21F, and required larger mainwheels and brakes, evidenced by slightly larger bulges in the fuselage; powerplant was the R-11-F2S, with a slightly higher augmented rating to retain high-speed performance at higher weights. The new aircraft entered production in 1961, as the MiG-21PF, and was codenamed 'Fishbed-D' by NATO.

Another new version, appearing at about the same time, was the MiG-21UTI conversion trainer. The airframe was a mixture of features, with the MiG-21F inlet – the trainer had no need for radar – the larger mainwheels of the MiG-21PF, and the pitot boom above the inlet as on the later all-weather fighter. The instructor's cockpit replaced a large part of the MiG-21's internal fuel capacity, so the

Above: The spine profile identifies this aircraft as a MiG-21bis, known to NATO as 'Fishbed-L'. This aircraft has a similar gunsight to the MiG-21MF; later versions have a true head-up display.

MiG-21UTI – 'Mongol-A' to NATO – had only a short endurance.

The MiG-21PF launched a rapid-fire process of development, in which the production configuration seemed to change almost every year. The history of the type, from this point, resembles a Russian novel: there are dozens of characters, each with a number of different names. In this case, the nomenclature is complicated by the NATO designation system, which reflects external changes rather than internal differences.

A PF development incorporating a further increase in fin chord, probably compensating for the larger nose, made its appearance in 1964. Just before that, it appears, the braking parachute was moved from the rear of the ventral fin to an acorn fairing at the base of the dorsal fin. In most aircraft, the tip of the fin incorporated a large plastic tip insert. The significance of this was that it covered the antenna for a high-capacity VHF communications and data link, known in various versions as ARL-S, RSIU and, in the West, Markham.

MiG-21PF 'Fishbed-E'

The importance of this data link was that it allowed the MiG-21 to be steered by ground controllers towards its target, whch in a high-speed intercept would be out of sight until the final seconds of an engagement. This version was regarded by the Soviet Union simply as a MiG-21PF, but was designated 'Fishbed-E' by NATO. The MiG-21US 'Mongol-B' was a trainer version with a similar fin.

The late-production MiG-21PF was quickly followed by two new versions, each of which introduced a single important change. The MiG-21PFS featured plain flaps, blown by air bled from the engine, in place of the original Fowler flaps. Takeoff performance may have suffered slightly, but the new arrangement reduced the approach and landing speed, and shortened the landing run. About the same time, a short-takeoff capability was added, by making provision for booster rockets on the sides of

Above: Standard MiG-21MF of the Soviet Air Force. One of the most widely produced single variants, the MiG-21MF was regarded as a true multi-purpose aircraft capable of air combat and strike missions.

Below: Another MiG-21MF, photographed on the same occasion as the example illustrated above. An unusual feature of these individuals is that the inboard wing pylons have been removed.

Right: Two MiG-21MFs in long-range trim with three external tanks. The 'wet' outer pylons of the third-generation MiG-21s added some 30 per cent to the maximum usable fuel capacity of the type.

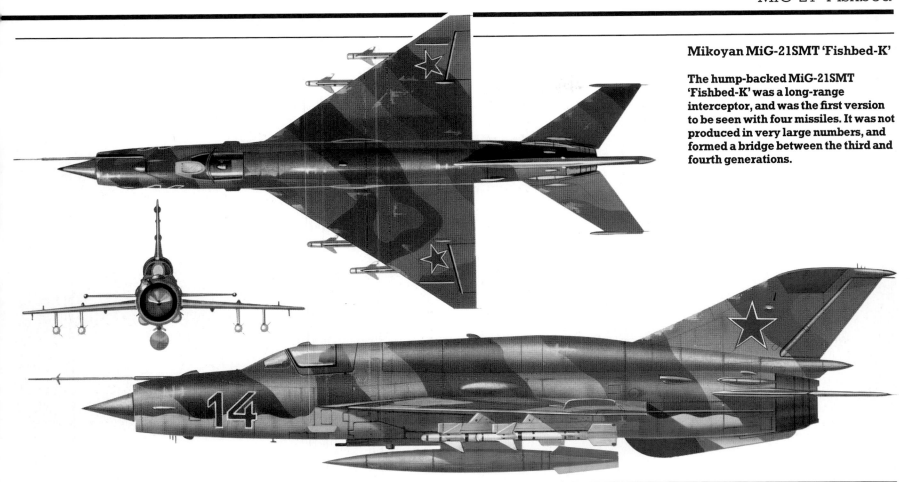

Mikoyan MiG-21SMT 'Fishbed-K'

The hump-backed MiG-21SMT 'Fishbed-K' was a long-range interceptor, and was the first version to be seen with four missiles. It was not produced in very large numbers, and formed a bridge between the third and fourth generations.

the fuselage. As this version was virtually indistinguishable from its predecessor, it was also known as 'Fishbed-E' in the NATO system.

The late-production MiG-21PF formed the basis of the first MiG-21 variant to be built in India. Designated MiG-21FL, it was a combination of old and new features, with the MiG-21PF airframe and the uprated R-11-F2S-300 engine (see below). Like other export versions of the aircraft, it carried the R2L 'Spin Scan-B' radar, a cheaper and less capable modification of the R1L designed for exports and wartime production. It entered production at Hindustan Aeronautics Limited's specially built Nasik plant, near Bombay, around 1967-68, while the R-11 was built at Koraput. The HAL-built aircraft were also equipped to take a locally manufactured ventral pack housing a GSh-23 cannon (see below) and 150 rounds of ammunition; the pack was attached to the centreline pylon.

Observed at almost the same time as the PFS was the MiG-21PFM, distinguished by its conventional, separate windshield and sideways-hinged canopy and known to NATO as 'Fishbed-F'. It is probable that the main reason for the change was to improve the effectiveness of the ejection system; the time required to hinge the canopy forwards, as opposed to blowing it off, and the delay while the seat and canopy separated, must have increased the minimum safe altitude for ejection. The PFM is also thought to have introduced the R-11-F2S-300, with a further 5 per cent thrust increase.

The next phase in development almost certainly reflected combat experience in Vietnam. The MiG-21PF had proved useful, but the MiG-17 had been, if anything, more successful; the more modern fighter had a poor endurance, its radar was not good enough to be a major improvement, and – crucially – it had no guns. The solution to many of these problems was found in a quite extensive redesign of the MiG-21, which began to enter service in 1968.

The basic airframe of the new MiG-21PFMA was similar to that of the PFM. The dorsal spine, however, was enlarged once again, with a straight top line and a wider base; this change was not hard to implement, since the dorsal spine is a secondary fairing structure, added to the fuselage in the last stages of construction. The spine is not believed to contain any fuel, with the possible exception of a small header tank to provide the engine with a back-up gravity feed. Instead, the spine is used to contain avionics and ancillary equipment, possibly including a gas- or battery-powered emergency power unit.

The other main external change on the PFMA was the addition of an extra pylon under each wing. These could be used for weapons, but were also plumbed to accept the same 108gal (490lit) tanks as the centreline pylon. The PFMA could therefore carry twice as much ordnance as earlier versions, or could be configured with a much greater operational radius.

Most PFMAs featured another significant change: the return of the internal gun. This was the GSh-23, successfully developed within extremely tight restrictions on space and weight. Its design was based on the Gast principle, devised in Germany during the 1939-45 war; it incorporated two side-by-side barrels, with their firing mechanisms coupled by a horizontal rocker arm so that the recoil energy of one barrel was used to cock and fire the other one.

The system was extremely light, weighing only 130lb (60kg) without ammunition, required no external power and imposed low recoil forces on the airframe. Together with 200 rounds of 23mm high-explosive/incendiary ammunition, it fitted neatly into a small space in the belly of the MiG-21. The equipment previously housed in that position – possibly a battery, or the oxygen system – was presumably relocated in the enlarged spine. Because of the weapon's small size, the ventral drop tank could still be carried; the splayed-out ammunition chutes protruding from the gun-pack kept the spent cases away from the tank. Another external feature associated with the gun was the small strake beneath each blow-in auxiliary inlet, designed to prevent the ingestion of gun gas.

GSh-23 performance

The GSh-23 was also notable for the shortness of its twin barrels. In gun design, a key parameter is the barrel length expressed as a multiple of the calibre. The Gsh-23 barrels are only 40 calibres long, while most aircraft cannon measure 70 calibres or more. The statistics for the GSh-23, as reported in the West, appear to be impressive: the weapon fires a 6.35oz (180g) projectile and is said to have an 'effective range' of 2,950-3,300ft (950-1,000m) and a 3,000rds/min rate of fire. But its true effectiveness is hard to assess without knowing its muzzle velocity, which must be limited by its barrel length, and dispersion, both of which are crucial in determining the amount of energy that the gun can put on to its target. In any event, the combat record of the later MiG-21s does not appear to show the substantial proportion of gun kills that show up in Western claims of the same period.

Codenamed 'Fishbed-J' by NATO, this third-generation development of the MiG-21 was also produced in India, as the MiG-21M; production at Nasik started in 1970. In the Soviet Union, however, it was quite rapidly super-

seded by the MiG-21MF, powered by the new Tumansky R-13-300. An increase of nearly 20 per cent in unreheated thrust, coupled with a slight reduction in engine weight – probably achieved through the greater use of titanium alloys – significantly improved the fighter's all-round performance, and probably made the full five-pylon capacity more useful in practical operations. To NATO, the MiG-21M and MiG-21MF were also 'Fishbed-J', being externally similar to the MiG-21PFMA. The MiG-21UM 'Mongol-C' was the trainer equivalent.

Avionics changes on the MiG-21MF included a modified R1L radar operating in J-band, and accordingly named 'Jay Bird' by NATO. It probably included a ranging function for use with the GSh-23. The MiG-21MF also featured an improved air-data system – evidenced by a yaw-rate sensor on the nose boom and a pitch sensor on the port side of the nose – which may have been associated with newly introduced autostabilization equipment or a simple bomb-aiming computer.

The third-generation MiG-21 was also adapted for the tactical reconnaissance role, in a number of slightly different versions; like snowflakes, no two seem to be quite alike, and NATO sidesteps the issue by referring to them all generically as 'Fishbed-H'. One version, designated MiG-21R and operated by Egypt, features a camera pack built into the belly, replacing the GSh-23 installation and other avionics behind the nosewheel bay. The pack contains oblique and vertical cameras.

Another type is operated by Soviet and Warsaw Pact forces, and is believed

Below: Points of interest on the very powerful R-25 engine – this is a HAL-built example – include the neatly packaged accessories and the engine's simplicity: there is no variable geometry whatsoever.

Below: The rear fuselage of the MiG-21bis, looking aft from the transport break joint. Auxiliary air ducts are visible. Note the deeper, stronger frames around the final jetpipe, which carry the tailplane loads.

Bottom: The MiG-21bis line at Nasik. Note that the spine is one of the last elements added to the basic fuselage structure, which is common to all MiG-21s. An in-service MiG-21M is being overhauled on the left.

to be designated MiG-21RF; it carries an external reconnaissance pod on the centreline pylon and different pods configured for optical and electronic reconnaissance have been observed. It has no gun and no anti-ingestion strakes, and a conduit connects the gun-bay area with the sensor pod. Small antennas, probably connected with an electronic support measures (ESM) listening system, are fitted to the wingtips. A large antenna is built into the dorsal spine, and is probably a downlink through which real-time information can be transmitted to a ground station or relay aircraft; this capability has been attributed to the MiG-21RF by USAF sources.

The last of the third-generation MiG-21s was something of an oddity. Observed in 1971, it was readily distinguished by a still fatter dorsal spine, which now sported a slightly convex top line peaking level with the wing trailing edge. The hunchbacked aircraft was the MiG-21SMT, known to NATO as 'Fishbed-K', and there is no reasonable doubt that the MiG-21SMT's spine contains extra fuel, to extend the range of the aircraft. Despite this attempt at curing one of the type's main shortcomings, the MiG-21SMT was not exported outside the Soviet Union, and was replaced in production by models which approximated to the earlier aerodynamic shape.

The explanation probably lay in changing requirements. The MiG-21PFMA was equipped to carry a four-

missile armament, but in fact it very seldom did so in service, and neither did the MiG-21MF. The likely reason was that the weight and drag of the extra missiles reduced the fighter's endurance, which was short enough in any case, to an unacceptable level, and the SMT was designed to rectify the situation. The internal layout of the spine is not known, but it is likely that avionics and ancillary equipment were installed in the forward part, with some 60-100gal (270-450lit) of extra fuel to the rear. Given the normal rule of thumb that half the fuel in an external tank is used to propel the tank through the air, the SMT's extra internal fuel was roughly equivalent to the two extra tanks that could be carried by the MiG-21PFMA and subsequent aircraft.

In any case, the MiG-21SMT was the first version of the type to be depicted carrying four missiles; the outboard pair were usually of a new type, known as the AA-2-2 'Advanced Atoll' and combining the standard AA-2 airframe and motor with a semi-active radar-homing guidance system. In theory, the AA-2-2 could function outside visual range, but in practice is more likely to have been designed for use outside the IR missile's effective envelope, in beam or collision-course attacks. A similar variant of the Sidewinder, the AIM-9C, was developed in the USA, but enjoyed little success, being withdrawn from service before it was used in combat. Whether the AA-2-2 is more useful is not known.

The modifications to the MiG-21SMT may have adversely affected the speed or manoeuvrability of the aircraft. However, it was outside factors that would shape the development of the MiG-21 family in the early 1970s. The USAF had digested its own Vietnam lessons, and was developing the new F-15. The McDonnell Douglas fighter promised great advances in flight perform-

Right: A Soviet MiG-21bis 'Fishbed-L', seen here with its optional armament of two IR-homing AA-2 'Atoll' and two radar-homing AA-2-2 'Advanced Atoll' air-to-air missiles.

Mikoyan MiG-21Mbis 'Fishbed-N'

The most heavily armed MiG-21bis variant carries AA-2-2s outboard and AA-8s inboard. This aircraft carries no centreline tank, suggesting a very short mission radius.

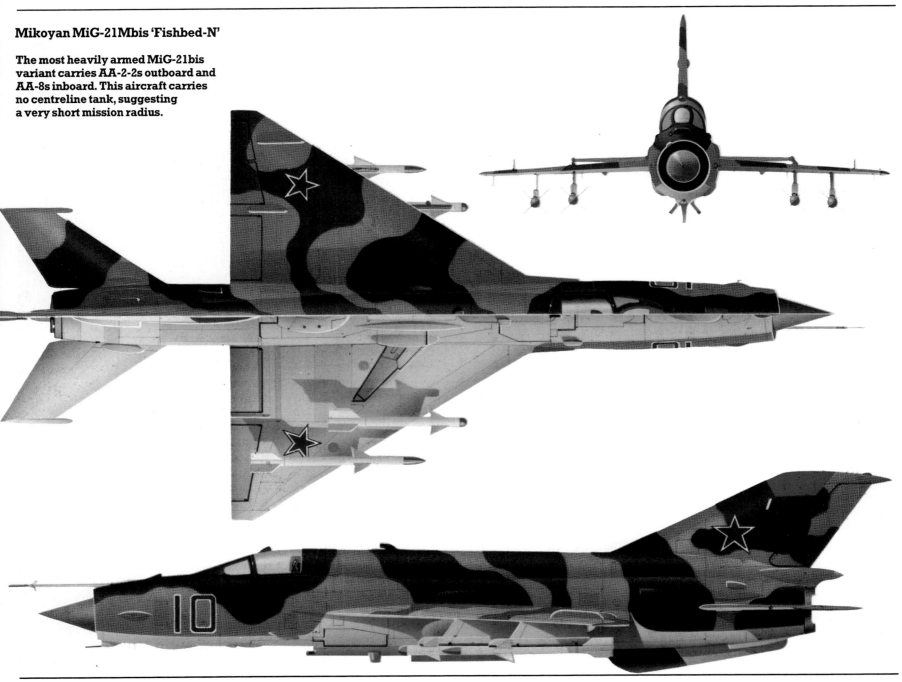

Below: Despite its poor quality, this photograph, released by the US DoD and State Department in March 1985, shows that Cuba has received the updated MiG-21bis, with its generally improved combat capability.

Above: The arrival of MiG-21Fs in Cuba in November 1962, revealed in this USAF reconnaissance photo, pushed US-Soviet relations closer to the crisis point, despite the limited capacity of those aircraft.

Above: Nearly a quarter-century later, MiG-21s in Cuba were still regarded as a threat. This reconnaissance photo of San Julian airfield was released by the US State Department in early 1985.

Below: A once-unthinkable formation: an F-16 and an A-10 of Tactical Air Command with a MiG-21 and a MiG-15UTI. The Soviet aircraft are in Egyptian service; the occasion was the Bright Star 82 joint exercise.

ance, and would pose a significant threat to Soviet airpower. Meanwhile, the MiG-23 was being prepared for service, and would be available in large quantities from 1971-72. The MiG-23 had excellent range, even with four missiles, but was not as agile as the MiG-21.

Apparently, the Soviet armed forces decided to field a mixed force of MiG-23s assigned to the long-range fighter and escort missions, and MiG-21s dedicated to the tactical air defence role. Extended range was no longer a priority for the MiG-21, but higher performance and improved equipment were desirable. The result was the fourth and final generation of MiG-21s.

The final generation

The first of these was the MiG-21bis, which entered production in the early 1970s, but which was not publicly reported until 1978, when it was offered to Finland. The MiG-21bis resembles the MiG-21MF very closely, and it requires careful scrutiny to see that the dorsal spine has been modified once again, reducing drag and accommodating a larger header tank. Internally, too, the airframe is reported to be revised and strengthened, increasing internal fuel capacity, and the avionics are improved. It is known to NATO as 'Fishbed-L'.

The new model was closely followed by the very similar MiG-21Mbis 'Fishbed-N' (the '-M' suffix is not used, because of possible confusion), distinguished by two small antennas, each resembling a miniature bow and arrow, on the nose and tail; these are usually stated to be associated with a new instrument landing system, standard on all Soviet

types in the 1970s and known as 'Swift Rod.'

The most important change, however, was introduced after the MiG-21bis had entered production: the use of a completely new engine, the Tumansky R-25. Originally believed to be rated at 16,500lb (7,500kg) thrust, it is now known to produce over 19,800lb (9,000kg) with full afterburner, 36 per cent more than the R-13; the lightweight MiG-21bis, therefore, has only 20 per cent less thrust than the much larger F-16. The R-25 has the highest thrust/weight ratio of any pure-jet engine in service, being no heavier than the R-13.

The thrust increase has been made possible by a number of changes. The R-25 appears to have one more compressor stage than the R-11 and R-13; the mechanical and aerodynamic design of the compressor has been improved, and more advanced materials have presumably been used. Unreheated thrust is probably some 20 per cent higher than that of the R-13-300. The augmentor, however, is completely new, and gives

Left: MiG-21PFs were the main subtype used in North Vietnam; had a cannon-equipped version been available earlier, the Vietnamese pilots might have been even more successful in air-to-air combat against their USAF and US Navy adversaries.

the new engine an augmentation ratio (the ratio of augmented thrust to dry thrust) of 1.5:1, compared with 1.3:1 for the R-13. The new augmenter is also claimed to provide better handling at high altitude.

The late-model MiG-21bis has a revised cockpit, with a head-up display (HUD) replacing the prominent head-down scope of earlier versions. It also carries the R-60 (known to NATO as the AA-8 'Aphid') missile originally developed for the MiG-23. The R-60 is an unusual weapon, optimized for high-g manoeuvrability rather than range; it is much smaller than the AA-2 or Sidewinder. It is not believed to have an all-aspect capability, but its high agility gives it an expanded firing envelope against manoeuvring targets at short range. Paired with the radar-guided AA-2-2, it makes up an effective armament combination.

In 1979 the MiG-21bis and R-25 entered production in India, and about 120 had been built by 1984. Indian sources officially describe the aircraft as 'the last of the MiG-21 series'; there has been no sign of any further development of the MiG-21 in the Soviet Union, and production of the type is declining in favour of newer fighters. Quite possibly, the Xian J-7 will be the last member of the family in production by 1986-87.

Exactly how many MiG-21s were built is hard to assess, but there is little doubt that the total has easily topped the record of just over 5,000 set by the F-4 Phantom. A study of the size of the worldwide MiG-21 fleet – which probably peaked at about 5,000 aircraft in the mid-1970s – combined with some allowance for combat losses, attrition and the replacement of obsolete variants, suggests that about 6,500-7,000 MiG-21s of all types have been built in the Soviet Union. HAL has built about 400, and a similar quantity of 'bootlegged' J-7s have come out of the Xian facility. Czech production was probably on a smaller scale, with perhaps 200 aircraft being delivered in the early 1960s. The grand total of 7,500-8,000 deliveries makes the MiG-21 the most widely built of all supersonic combat aircraft.

'MiG diplomacy'

It was the MiG-21 that brought the phrase 'MiG diplomacy' into the international lexicon. Many newly independent or post-revolutionary countries received a small unit of MiG-21s at a subsidized price, on excellent terms and with payment in their own currency. Many saw little, if any, use: Indonesia's MiG-21Fs lay idle for many years after a political rift interrupted the spares supply. The type was, however, standard equipment for Middle Eastern and North African allies of the Soviet Union, and in most cases still made up the bulk of their fleets in 1985. Neither was 'MiG diplomacy' quite dead: the mere rumour that MiG-21s were on their way to Nicaragua in late 1983 caused a US reaction which, in the opinion of some observers, would have been more appropriate for the arrival of a regiment of Backfires.

The MiG-21 has been delivered to more nations than any other supersonic fighter, and has fought in virtually every major conflict since it entered service. Western assessments of its qualities have varied widely: at times, it has been condemned as being useless for any mission more demanding than the Liberation Day flypast; at other times, it has been used as a reference point for an

Left: The MiG-21 is the world's most widely built and widely used supersonic fighter. Egypt, in particular, has used nine different subtypes, while those supplied to North Vietnam saw extensive action.

Egyptian Air Force Mig-21PF 'Fishbed-D'

Egyptian Air Force MiG-21PF 'Fishbed-E'

Egyptian Air Force MiG-21RF 'Fishbed-H'

Egyptian Air Force MiG-21MF 'Fishbed-J'

North Vietnamese Air Force MiG-21PFMA 'Fishbed-J'

Right: Non-Soviet pilots have praised the MiG-21 for its straightforward handling and ruggedness. In this ground-to-air photograph an Indian pilot shows off a specially marked display aircraft.

entire generation of fighter development. The truth does not lie between these two viewpoints, because both of them are accurate.

If flight performance and handling make a fighter, the MiG-21 has stayed near the top of the heap for more than two decades. The design has no basic handling vices, and can be pushed to its aerodynamic limits without courting a violent departure from controlled flight. This is mainly due to the delta wing, which is highly resistant to stalling; instead of suffering an abrupt break-up of the airflow, leading to the loss of aileron control, a sudden wing drop and a spin, the delta can exploit this attribute to a greater extent than a conventional tailless configuration. Because of its long tail arm, it is more stable in yaw and has more control power in pitch. Another reason for the MiG-21's tractability and tolerance of abuse is the nose inlet, which is free from all airframe effects and feeds the engine efficiently even at high angles of attack.

Handling limitations
The main limitation on handling is that the drag of the delta builds up much more quickly than the lift, so the MiG-21 must lose either speed or height when it pulls a sharp manoeuvre. At Mach 0.9 and 15,000ft (4,570m), even the F-4E can sustain a turn rate 20 per cent faster than the MiG-21MF, and the F-16 and F-15 are in a completely different class. However, the MiG-21's instantaneous turn rate – the highest rate it can generate, irrespective of whether it loses speed or height – is virtually equal to that of the F-4E at Mach 0.9, and much better at Mach 0.5, at which speed the MiG-21 can use its flaps to improve its manoeuvre performance. Clearly, the answer for the MiG pilot is to avoid long tailchases, and concentrate on manoeuvres that combine abrupt turns with the opportunity to accelerate rapidly up to fighting speed. With the MiG-21bis – which has a thrust/weight ratio in the same class as the F-15 and F-16, combined with a low-drag airframe – this would be a particularly attractive tactic.

It should be noted, moreover, that the slatted F-4E, the F-15 and F-16 are by no means true contemporaries of the MiG-21. Direct contemporaries included the F-104 and Mirage, which were very much less manoeuvrable than the MiG, and the early F-4, which was subject to a highly dangerous stall-spin departure if flown beyond its limits.

Pilots have described the MiG-21 as a straightforward aircraft to fly. It seldom earns the description 'pleasant', probably because it has a rather basic artificial-feel system which leads to uncomfortably high stick forces. While there is autostabilization in pitch and roll, the pilot is mainly kept within the operating envelope by the artificial feel system, which provides very high stick forces at high airspeeds. One point in favour of the aircraft is the simplicity of its systems, which make the piloting task less complicated. Of all supersonic fighters, the MiG-21 is probably best suited to the inexperienced pilot.

Low-speed handling is particularly

Right: One modified MiG-21PFM airframe became the 'Fishbed-G', a low-speed, fixed-gear testbed for the jet-lift Stol concept and a predecessor of the 'Faithless' Stol fighter. Note down elevator on the approach.

good. The ailerons remain effective down to 130kt (240km/h), and the usual touchdown speed is about 140-145kt (260-270km/h). With the brake parachute used immediately on landing, the MiG-21 stops after a 1,320ft (400m) roll, providing a comfortable margin even on a short runway.

But flight performance and handling

are not everything. The MiG-21's best known drawback is basic to the design and resistant to easy fixes. Because of several design features – the minimal cross-section, the small volume of the wing and the location of the engine – virtually all the fuel is well ahead of the centre of gravity. As the fuel is burned, the aircraft becomes progressively

Above: Soviet Air Force MiG-21PFs participating in the 1967 Aviation Day display at Domodedovo.

Above right: The MiG-21 configuration was adapted for a series of larger aircraft, culminating in the Ye-166 testbed for high-Mach propulsion technology.

Below: In the early 1970s, the MiG-21MF was considered mature enough to let Western observers close to it, and it was used on goodwill exchange visits to France and Sweden. This gave the West its first close look at a Soviet combat aircraft – albeit a type which was no longer at the technological forefront.

more tail-heavy, until the centre of gravity passes outside limits and the aircraft becomes susceptible to a sudden, out-of-control pitch-up.

The severity of the problem varies from subtype to subtype; the R-13-powered aircraft, with a lighter engine, may be better off than the R-11-powered variants. Another factor may be piloting skill and qualifications – Soviet instructors probably teach foreign students to stay well away from the danger zone. However, the CG problem makes between 110 and 175gal (500-800lit) of the less than generous 570gal (2,540 lit) capacity unusable, and severely restricts the aircraft's endurance.

The other main problem is the spartan simplicity of the fighter's systems. As delivered, even the MiG-21MF lacked any navigation system other than a compass and basic beacon receivers, its gunsight toppled at 2.75g and it had no system for aiming bombs with any degree of accuracy. The 'Jay Bird' radar has a range of only 20 miles (32lm), and is masked by ground clutter below 3,000ft (915m) altitude. The MiG-21bis has a better cockpit, but still uses the antiquated 'Jay Bird' radar.

Western weapons and systems

A solution adopted by a number of operators has been to retrofit MiG-21s with improved systems, and Egypt, estranged from the Soviet Union, has gone farthest in this direction. The first step, in 1982, was to replace the K-13. This missile – at least in its export-standard model – is not the best of IR-homing weapons, and the Egyptian Air Force reckons to have doubled the effectiveness of its fleet by fitting the AIM-9P3 Sidewinder. (The AIM-9P3, too, is an export-standard weapon, and is not as capable as the legend-in-its-time AIM-9L.) Iraq has followed suit, clearing its MiG-21s to fire the Matra 550 Magic. Meanwhile, Egypt's MiG-21MFs are being further upgraded with the Emerson APQ-159 radar, similar to that of the F-5E, British GEC Avionics head-up displays, and provision for the medium-range AIM-7F Sparrow missile. Emerson is prime contractor, and the first modified aircraft was due to start ground tests in mid-1985, and to fly in early 1986.

Ferranti and Smiths Industries have also developed combined head-up display and weapon-aiming computer systems (Hudwacs) for retrofit to small combat aircraft, including the MiG-21. Most such contracts are regarded as highly confidential; however, India is definitely a target, and China is offering the J-7M, a J-7 with British avionics. Ferranti has announced a new radar named Red Fox, designed to replace 'Jay Bird'. A repack-

MiG-21 was clearly superior in a close fight to the early F-4, having the edge in visibility and manoeuvrability, and the MiG-21 remained a dangerous adversary throughout the war.

The inability to sustain air superiority over the theatre to the extent which had been possible in Korea came as a shock to the USAF, and had a number of consequences. The slatted wing of the F-4E was a short-term counter to the MiG-21; for smaller allied nations, the USAF launched development of the F-5E, designed to emulate the MiG-21's performance. Finally, air-to-air dogfight performance became the key parameter in the new US fighters of the 1970s.

Debut in the Middle East

The MiG-21's debut in the Middle East theatre was unexpectedly cancelled on June 6, 1967. Egypt's apparently formidable fleet of MiG-21s was a priority target for Israel's meticulously devastating air-strike that morning, and not one made it into the air. The aircraft were replaced by the end of 1968, and air battles resumed in March 1969. Seven Egyptian MiG-21s were claimed in a single battle in September 1969, and the Israeli Air Force began to make increasingly bold incursions into Egyptian airspace.

In late January the Soviet Union moved a complete Soviet-manned air defence organization into Egypt, including the new MiG-21MF 'Fishbed-J' fighters. The Soviet force, according to Israeli sources, included 72 MiG-21MFs drawn from Frontal Aviation assets in Hungary. Confrontation was inevitable, and the IAF launched attacks on Soviet radar and missile sites in early July. On July 30, two F-4s and two Mirages on an armed reconnaissance mission engaged a group of a dozen MiG-21MFs, claiming five kills without loss. The victory was ascribed to the lack of experience shown by the Soviet pilots, and to the Israelis' use of the new and secret Rafael Shafrir missile, then among the best weapons in its class. Compared to the contemporary export-model Sidewinder, or the K-13, the Shafrir was more reliable and could be fired over a wider manoeuvring envelope.

aged version of the Sea Harrier FRS.1 radar, Red Fox would provide much better air-to-air performance, and could also be used for air-to-sea search. There is even a possibility of an entire engine change, both the GE F404 and the PW1120 having been studied. However, this would be very expensive, as either engine probably costs more than a new J-7.

One final attribute of the MiG-21 is its sheer ease of operation. It embodies the Soviet philosophy of simplicity and ruggedness; nothing on the aircraft is not absolutely essential, and considerable attention has been given to ensuring that routine flight-line activities such as rearming and inspection are easy, and require a minimum of equipment. The fighter is regarded as highly reliable, and can be turned round between missions in ten minutes.

The best way of summing up the MiG-21 is probably to say that it has a mix of good and bad qualities, but that it carries them to greater extremes than most other fighters. In combat, it has been demonstrated that the MiG-21 is very effective when the situation permits tactics which exploit its good attributes, but suffers severely when the tables are turned and the adversary's tactics are aimed at its weak spots.

India and Vietnam

The first potential use of the MiG-21 in combat was a non-event. India had received six MiG-21Fs in February 1963, followed by another 24 aircraft in 1964-65, but when war broke out between India and Pakistan in September 1965, only 10 aircraft were believed to be operational. The use of the MiG-21 was sporadic, and the only reported encounter involved a Pakistan Air Force F-104 which encountered four MiG-21s when at the limit of its endurance. The PAF pilot used the F-104's speed to outrun the MiG-21s on the deck. The Indian Air Force also tried to intercept the PAF's single RB-57F reconnaissance-bomber, but its high altitude frustrated their efforts.

The Vietnam theatre, where the MiG-21PF arrived at the end of 1965, was near-ideal for the Soviet fighter. The mis-

sion was air defence over a relatively small area, and the fighters were working within a Soviet-supplied system that also included acquisition radars, surface-to-air missiles and the control systems to tie them all together. The MiG pilots were scrambed as needed, and vectored accurately towards their targets by ground control. The US Air Force and Navy strike aircraft and escorts were operating at long range, and their endurance over the target was limited.

Other factors favoured the North Vietnamese pilots. The US pilots were not permitted to launch missiles without positive visual identification, a restriction which not only rendered the radar and medium-range missiles of the Phantom

Above: Yugoslav Air Force MiG-21PFMAs – the examples shown here are early models without an internal gun – in a tunnel-type underground hangar. More often, MiG-21s are protected by dispersal and their ability to use sod runways.

of little use, but if anything left the MiG-21 at an advantage; because the MiG-21 was smaller than the F-4, and had a less smoky engine, the MiG-21 pilot could visually identify an F-4 long before an F-4 pilot could identify the MiG. The MiG pilots also had quite limited objectives. If they could jump the incoming strike aircraft and force them to dump their weapons, they had succeeded. Finally, as noted above, the

Right: India has both built and operated a variety of MiG-21s, including these HAL-built MiG-21Ms.

In the 1973 Middle East war, the EAF used its MiG-21s for close support, (armed with rockets and 550lb (250kg) bombs) as well as for battlefield air superiority. Because of the extensive use of SAMs, air combat was largely confined to very low altitudes and, very often, to low airspeeds. The MiG-21's low-speed performance was extensively used, and the gun was regarded as the main air-combat weapon – some early MiG-21PFMAs were retrofitted with the GSh-23 during the war. The EAF claimed to have held its own in the conflict, particularly in air-to-air actions, but – once again – the Shafrir was a powerful factor on the Israeli side.

Since 1973, the MiG-21 has been used in combat by Iraq, in the largely hidden war against Iran, and by Syria. The Syrian-Israeli conflicts will be discussed in the chapter on the MiG-23; to avoid repetition, it will suffice to say that the technical quality of the MiG-21 was not a major issue.

Overall, the MiG-21 has qualified itself as a classic design. Despite its age, it remains a very credible dogfighter. Even now, a late-model MiG-21, with updated electronics and effective weapons, could be one of the most cost-effective combat aircraft on the market.

Right: A mixed formation of two MiG-21R reconnaissance fighters (second and third from camera) and two escorting MiG-21MFs, all of the Egyptian Air Force.

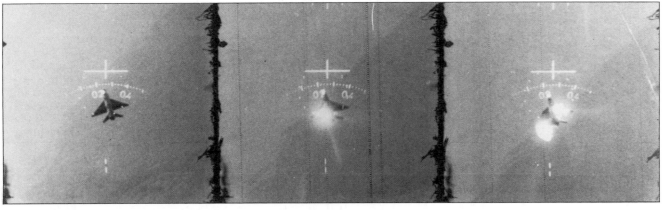

Left: In October 1973, a MiG-21 is destroyed by cannon fire from an Israeli F-4E Phantom. Despite good performance on paper, the Soviet fighter's own gun has not proved as lethal as the M61 carried by later models of the F-4.

Below: A mortally hit Egyptian MiG-21 falls in view of Israeli tank crews in 1973. The Israeli forces have a firm respect for MiG fighters, and – perhaps because of this – have consistently maintained high kill-to-loss ratios in combat.

MiG-23/27 'Flogger'

Few fighters of the 1960s have been built in such large numbers as the very fast and predatory-looking MiG family of swing-wing fighters that carry the NATO codename 'Flogger'. With no direct equivalent in the West, the MiG-23 and MiG-27 represent a uniquely Soviet approach to the tactical fighter problem: powerful, quite large and remarkably simple to build in quantity. It was the last of these qualities that shocked the West, making the types far more readily affordable than any Western fighter of comparable capability, and allowing them to be deployed with unprecedented speed.

In the early 1960s, it seemed that almost every air arm in the world was taking delivery of new and advanced equipment. Genuine Mach 2 performance, the province of a very few aircraft in the late 1950s, was beginning to reach the squadrons. In the Frontal Aviation inventory, the MiG-21 was well established in production, the radar-equipped versions were entering service, and the merits and deficiencies of the type were clearly appreciated in the Soviet Union if not in the West.

Western fighters of the 1960s thoroughly outclassed their Soviet counterparts, not only in payload and range but also in operational equipment: more effective air-to-air missiles, carried in larger numbers; air-to-air radars large enough to detect and track targets beyond visual range, and guide missiles on to them; improved navigation equipment permitting routine operations beyond the range of ground control. The pinnacle of fighter design at that time was the US Navy's new F-4 Phantom: compared with the contemporary MiG-21PF, the Phantom carried four times as many missiles and eight times as many bombs, could pick up targets three or four times as far away and, in theory, could shoot them down before coming within range of their weapons.

While the supremacy of numbers is paramount in Soviet military doctrine, the related discipline of 'military-technical art' concerns the technical quality of military equipment. It involves the identification of the most important factors in weapon performance, and the standards which must be met to ensure that an opponent does not enjoy some

overwhelming advantage due to technology. At the same time, military-technical studies single out performance standards which are less important, and can be sacrificed in the interests of easy production.

It was clear in the early 1960s that some of the deficiencies of the existing MiG-21 could become critical by the end of the decade. An aircraft in the class of the F-4 would have some vital advantages: the 'first look', because of its radar, the 'first shot', because of its long-range missiles, and, importantly, the ability to accept or decline an engagement, because of its higher performance. Against the MiG-21, the F-4 would be able to fight when the circumstances were favourable and show discretion at other times. It should be noted that in Vietnam, the MiG-21 showed up well when circumstances were in its favour; on the few occasions when F-4 units mounted an aggressive fighter sweep, the kill-to-loss ratio was heavily in favour of the F-4.

As the new fighter requirement made

its way through the system, this type of comparison helped define the most important qualities of a new type. A basic building block was the ability to detect and engage targets beyond visual range (BVR), calling for a long-range search and tracking radar and reliable radar-guided missiles. Like the F-4, the new fighter would carry shorter-range IR-homing missiles for close combat.

Performance requirements

The new type was to be faster in level flight, climb and acceleration than the MiG-21, while greater range would also be desirable; although no dramatic increase in the internal fuel capacity, as a fraction of clean gross weight, was demanded, it could be assumed that the MiG-21's CG problem would be avoided and general advances in design would provide a further improvement. The MiG-21 was judged correctly to be more manoeuvrable than most of its contemporaries, so no increase in sustained or instantaneous turn rates was required.

Above: A MiG-23M and flight-suited aircrew photographed at a base in the cis-Carpathian Military District. The aircraft carries a centreline fuel tank, with very little ground clearance on this version.

Right: An excellent sequence showing the first swing-wing MiG, the Ye-231 (or Ye-23-1). The original and much cleaner configuration of the prototype is clearly visible.

Below: The MiG-21DPD was strictly a low-speed test aircraft, with a fixed landing gear. The lightweight, compact lift engines were probably developed by the Kolesov bureau.

Below: The MiG-21DPD was part of a complete V/Stol technology programme. Together with the Yak-36, it led to the operational Yak-38, as well as the Ye-230 prototype.

Soviet V/Stol fighter development

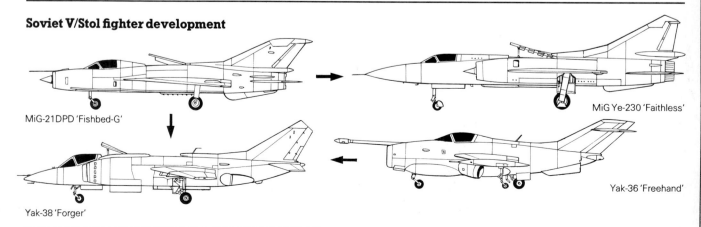

MiG-21DPD 'Fishbed-G'

MiG Ye-230 'Faithless'

Yak-38 'Forger'

Yak-36 'Freehand'

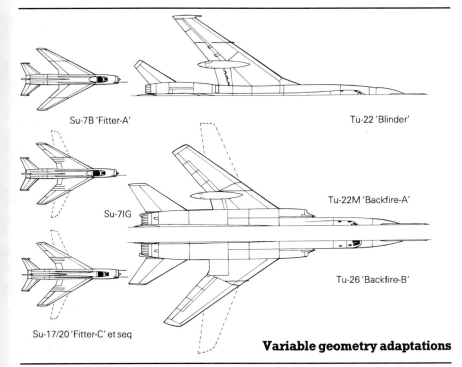

Su-7B 'Fitter-A'

Tu-22 'Blinder'

Su-7IG

Tu-22M 'Backfire-A'

Su-17/20 'Fitter-C' et seq

Tu-26 'Backfire-B'

Variable geometry adaptations

Above: One TsAGI VG configuration was intended for adaptations of existing aircraft, such as the Su-7 and Tu-22. The Su-7IG and Tu-22M test/evaluation types led to the definitive Su-17/20 series and the Tu-26.

Below: The wing of the Ye-231 prototype was cleaner and smaller than that of the subsequent production aircraft; the main part of the vertical fin was the same size, but the dorsal fin was noticeably smaller.

Field performance was also pegged at MiG-21 levels. The final requirement was – as usual – that the size and cost of the aircraft be kept to a minimum. The requirement was probably issued by the TsKB in late 1963 or early 1964.

It must have been clear that the requirement would probably have to be met by a new aircraft. The most advanced Soviet fighters under development were the PVO's new interceptors, the Mikoyan Ye-26 (MiG-25) and the Sukhoi Su-15. The Mach 3, short-range MiG-25 was far too specialized for the FA, and while the Su-15 might have seemed superficially close to the requirement in terms of flight performance, capacity for avionics and weapons and size, it was a specialized PVO weapon. Its radar was optimized for counter-countermeasures performance rather than range, it was heavily dependent on maintenance facilities and it needed too long a runway. The same objections applied to the series of tailed-delta MiG prototypes developed between 1959 and 1962.

The requirement was tougher than it might appear at first sight. The speed and payload targets, coupled with a limitation on field lengths, eliminated the straightforward tailed delta. The classic Western compromise would have been a thin-section, moderately swept wing, as on the F-4, Mirage F.1 and Crusader. The MiG OKB was already developing an aircraft, the Ye-26, with such a wing, but it does not seem to have been considered for very long in the case of the new FA aircraft. The reason for this probably lies in the basic design trades: the speed requirement would have driven the wing loading upward to the point where the field-length target was out of reach.

The solution was to evaluate what were, at the time, two radically new technologies which promised to relieve the aerodynamic problems involved in attaining high speeds without long runways. One was variable sweep, the other was propulsive lift.

The latter, as applied to a basically conventional supersonic fighter, was not

New variable geometry fighters

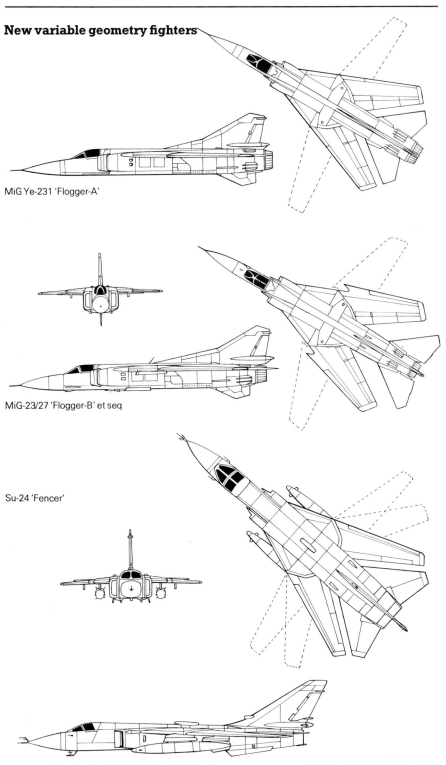

MiG Ye-231 'Flogger-A'

MiG-23/27 'Flogger-B' et seq

Su-24 'Fencer'

Left: This view shows clearly how the prototype's stabilizer, further forward than that of the production aircraft, fits neatly into the overall planform so that the wing and stabilizer tips align when the wing is in the fully swept position with the leading edge at an angle of 72°.

Above: TsAGI developed a neat planform for new VG aircraft such as the Ye-231, which featured a simple wing/fuselage junction and, unlike most Western layouts, had room for a high-capacity stores pylon under the glove. Modified for the production MiG-23, it was retained for the Su-24.

quite unique to the Soviet Union, being evaluated almost in parallel by Saab in the early days of the Viggen programme. The fighter would be equipped with two or three small lift jets mounted vertically in the fuselage, slightly forward of the CG and exhausting through variable louvres in the belly. On takeoff and landing, these engines would provide a vertical thrust equal to between a third and a half of the total weight of the aircraft, reducing the need for lift. All things being equal, the aircraft would take off and land more slowly.

There was a further benefit. As the speed of an aircraft is reduced from its maximum, it is given more 'up elevator' to raise the nose, increase the wing's angle of attack and maintain lift for level flight. The elevator (or stabilizer) is generating an increasing amount of downward thrust, and the wings have to provide more lift to compensate for this force. Supersonic combat aircraft tend to have short tails, for reasons of weight and drag. The stabilizer is working with a short lever, and the downforce must be higher; look at any supersonic combat aircraft on take-off or on the approach, and you can see the stabilizer angled sharply nose-down, and thrusting the whole aircraft towards the ground.

In the jet-lift-assisted fighter, the lift-jets would provide a powerful and drag-free force to raise the nose, being ahead of the CG. At low speeds, the stabilizer could actually be used to lift the tail, and yet the aircraft would remain stable. In effect, the lift-jets allowed the area of the stabilizer to be added to that of the wing, rather than subtracted from it. The potential reduction in landing and takeoff speed was very large indeed, and – apart from the extra internal

Right: MiG-23U trainers are attached to each operational regiment. They have a back-up combat mission, but are compromised operationally by having a much less effective radar than the single-seat variants.

Below right: Photographed around 1975, this MiG-23M has a full complement of operational equipment including the IRST (infra-red search and track) set under the nose. The black panel ahead of the IRST forestalls reflection problems.

Below: The basically clean and straightforward lines of the MiG-23 – a direct result of the Soviet emphasis on ease of production – are very apparent on what appears to be a factory-fresh MiG-23M.

volume occupied by the lift engines – the fighter could retain an uncompromised supersonic configuration with a small-area, low-drag wing and no complex high-lift devices.

The other formula considered for the new FA fighter, variable sweep, was more familiar in the West. TsAGI was entirely familiar with the history of variable sweep, although it had never been tested in the Soviet Union. The concept was little younger than the swept wing itself, having first studied as soon as the unfavourable low-speed characteristics of the swept wing were detected. It had been tried on two manned aircraft in the USA, with indifferent results, mainly because it was thought necessary to slide the entire wing root fore and aft to keep the wing's aerodynamic centre in the same position.

British research work into Sir Barnes Wallis' Swallow concept pointed the way to eliminating this complication, by moving the pivot points away from the centreline and tapering the moving panels. Finally, in the late 1950s, John Stack's work at NASA's Langley Research Center showed that a fixed-root, outboard-pivot variable-sweep wing was within the state of the art and could be provided with effective aerodynamic controls.

Right: Even with the aid of top and side periscopes, the instructor's view from the MiG-23U rear cockpit is less than panoramic. Most performance monitoring is presumably carried out via instruments.

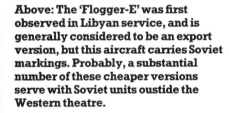

This work was thoroughly documented and discussed, and formed the starting point for TsAGI's investigations. Another source of inspiration was the General Dynamics F-111, revealed in mid-1964 but doubtless known to the Soviet Union before that time.

VG benefits

Although 'variable sweep' is an accurate description of the mechanical functioning of such a wing, some of its benefits and implications are connected with the fact that the aerodynamic shape of the wing changes in other ways as it swings back. The term coined by NASA – 'variable geometry' or VG – is not mere verbosity, but is more complete and accurate. The wing not only has variable sweep, but also variable span and variable thickness, all being significant.

Varying the sweep angle itself has certain benefits. Some high-lift devices work best on a virtually unswept wing. Highly swept wings, on the other hand, have some advantages: they have low drag at very high speeds, because the wing lies behind the main shock wave from the nose, and are relatively little affected by gusts in high-speed, low-level flight. Wings with more than 60° sweep have very poor low-speed behaviour, and such sweep angles are practical only with VG.

VG also means variable span. A long-span wing generates more lift for takeoff, and less induced drag – drag due to lift – in medium-speed cruising flight. At higher speeds, the drag due to the size of the wing, and Mach effects, become more important, and a shorter-span wing is more efficient. To some extent, too, a VG wing has variable area, because part of the trailing edge retracts into the fuselage or glove as it sweeps back. This increases the wing loading, reduces high-speed drag and improves the aircraft's low-level, high-speed ride.

As the wing sweeps back, its chord – measured parallel with the centreline – increases. Its physical thickness stays the same, so its aerodynamic thickness, defined as the ratio of thickness to chord, is reduced. Thick wings generate more lift at low speeds, thin wings produce less drag at high speeds, and the VG aircraft gets the best of both worlds again.

VG complications

It was these qualities that made VG attractive in the early 1960s, and made it the basis for so many design studies. Its implementation presented some challenges, however. Stability and control were complicated by the gross changes in aerodynamic shape: in particular, the aerodynamic centre (AC) of the aircraft tended to move aft with the sweeping of the wing, and moved further aft at supersonic speed, threatening to cause high trim drag. The rearward AC shift affected pitch stability as well, making the size and the position of the stabilizer more critical than ever. Lateral (roll) and directional (yaw) stability were also

Above: The 'Flogger-E' was first observed in Libyan service, and is generally considered to be an export version, but this aircraft carries Soviet markings. Probably, a substantial number of these cheaper versions serve with Soviet units oustide the Western theatre.

Below: Seen here undergoing pre-flight checks is another unusual specimen – a MiG-23M 'Flogger-B' with the large weapon shoes, and the dielectric head above the pylon, which are normally associated with strike versions of the type. It may be a development aircraft.

affected to some degree. Structurally, the chief problem was the design of small pivot mechanisms that would be completely reliable and yet would carry some of the highest loads in the airframe.

All the problems connected with AC shift could be reduced by moving the pivot points further outboard, and this also reduced the loads on the pivots because more of the flight loads were carried on the fixed part of the wing. But there were costs involved with this approach. Chiefly, the benefits of VG were reduced along with the risks.

TsAGI studies of these problems produced two different VG planforms. One was similar to that of the F-111, with a few variations which, without greatly affecting performance, made it easier to integrate into an aircraft design. The pivots were slightly farther apart, the distance between them being 22 per cent of the total span, rather than 17 per cent, and the maximum sweep angle, measured from the pivots, was slightly smaller.

As a result of these two differences, much less of the TsAGI wing actually retracted into the fuselage when it was swept back, and the fixed root or 'glove' was shorter than that on the F-111. This made the design of the fuselage less difficult, by reducing the size of the cut-out and cavity needed to accommodate the wing, made the glove shape compatible

Above: Ordnance fit on this MiG-23M appears to include dual AA-8 shoes, with provision for another store, under the gloves, an AA-2 shoe under the starboard belly pylon and a bomb rack to port.

with conventional inlets, and increased the span of the glove just enough to provide room for a high-capacity stores pylon. Another difference was a larger gap in plan view between the wings and the stabilizer, but like the F-111, and unlike later VG designs, the wings and sta-

bilizer were at the same level.

The other layout produced by TsAGI was originally intended for use on modified versions of swept-wing aircraft, and was based on an Su-7 planform, the pivots being set at 30 per cent span. This layout formed the basis for the Su-20/22 and the Tu-22M 'Backfire' bomber, both originally derived from fixed-geometry designs, but worked well enough to be adapted for the completely new Tupolev 'Blackjack' strategic bomber.

It was the more ambitious, F-111-style planform that was evaluated for the new

tactical fighter, alongside the propulsive-lift concept. The decision to do so was almost certainly taken during 1964, and represented a significant break with Western practice. In the West, VG was regarded as a feature of complex, expensive aircraft, and was used only where its perceived cost and complications were needed to meet specific mission requirements. TsAGI and the TsKB, however, intended to implement VG as cheaply as possible, using it to increase the mission efficiency of a basic tactical combat aircraft and thereby contain its size and cost.

Rival prototypes

Apparently, both MiG and Sukhoi OKBs were asked to build prototypes in response to the requirement. Sukhoi's aircraft was to be a short takeoff and landing (Stol) variant of the Su-15 interceptor, using jet lift, while Mikoyan was to build two tactical fighter prototypes, to test the jet-Stol concept and variable sweep in parallel. Mikoyan also adapted a MiG-21 airframe into the purely experimental MiG-21DPD 'Fishbed-G', for early tests of the concept.

At the same time, the Tumansky bureau started development of a new engine for the MiG types. Whether this engine is a turbojet or a turbofan has been disputed by different sources for

Mikoyan MiG-23MF 'Flogger-B' cutaway

1 Pitot tube
2 Radome
3 'High Lark' J-band radar scanner dish
4 Radar dish tracking mechanism
5 'Swift Rod' ILS antenna
6 Avionics cooling air scoop
7 Radar and avionics equipment bay
8 Ventral doppler antenna
9 Yaw vane
10 Dynamaic pressure probe (q-feel)
11 SRO-22 'Odd-Rods' IFF antenna
12 Armoured windscreen panel
13 Head-up display
14 Instrument panel shroud
15 Radar head-down display
16 Instrument panel
17 Rudder pedals
18 Angle of attack transmitter
19 IR sensor housing
20 Nosewheel steering unit
21 Torque scissor links
22 Pivoted axle beam
23 Twin aft-retracting nosewheels
24 Nosewheel spray/debris guard
25 Shock absorber strut
26 Nosehweel doors
27 Hydraulic retraction jack
28 Control column
29 Ejection seat firing handles
30 Wing sweep control lever
31 Engine throttle control lever
32 Pilot's ejection seat
33 Electrically-heated rearview mirror
34 Ejection seat headrest
35 Upward hingeing cockpit canopy cover
36 Canopy jack
37 Starboard air intake
38 Canopy hinge point
39 Screw-jack-actuated adjustable boundary layer splitter plate
40 Boundary layer bleed air holes
41 Port engine air intake
42 Intake internal flow fences
43 Retractable landing/taxying lamp (port and starboard)
44 Temperature probe
45 Variable-area intake ramp doors
46 Boundary layer bleed air ejector
47 Avionics equipment bay
48 ADF sense aerial
49 Boundary layer air duct
50 Forward fuselage fuel tank
51 Ventral cannon ammunition magazines
52 Ground power connections
53 Intake suction relief doors
54 Weapons system electronic control units
55 SO-69 Sirena 3 radar warning antennas
56 Fuselage flank fuel tanks
57 Wing glove fairing
58 Starboard Sirena 3 radar warning antennas
59 Jettisonable fuel tank (176Imp gal/800lit capacity)
60 Nose section of MiG-23U Flogger-C tandem-seat trainer
61 Student pilot's cockpit
62 Folding blind flying hood
63 Rear seat periscope (extended)
64 Instructor's cockpit
65 MiG-23BN Flogger-F dedicated ground attack variant
66 Radar ranging antenna
67 Laser ranger nose fairing
68 Raised cockpit canopy
69 Armoured fuselage side panels
70 Wing leading edge flap (lowered)
71 Starboard navigation light
72 Wing fully forward (16° sweep) position
73 Port wing integral fuel tank (total internal fuel capacity 1,265Imp gal/5,750lit)
74 Full span plain flap (lowered)
75 Starboard wing intermediate (45° sweep) position
76 Starboard wing full (72° sweep) position
77 Two-segment spoilers/lift dumpers
78 Non-swivelling jettisonable wing pylon (wing restricted to forward swept position)
79 Wing glove sealing plate
80 Wing pivot bearing
81 Wing pivot box carry-through unit (welded construction)
82 VHF antenna
83 Wing sweep control screw jacks
84 Fin root fillet
85 Rear fuselage fuel tank
86 Tumansky R-29B afterburning turbojet
87 Afterburner duct cooling air scoop
88 Cut-back fin root fillet (Flogger-G)
89 Tailplane control and hydraulic equipment bay
90 Starboard all-moving tailplane
91 Tailfin
92 Short wave ground control communications antenna
93 UHF antenna
94 ILS antenna
95 Sirena 3 tail warning radar
96 ECM antennas
97 Tail navigation light
98 Static discharger
99 Rudder
100 Rudder hydraulic actuators
101 Brake parachute housing
102 Split conic fairing parachute door
103 Variable area afterburner nozzle
104 Fixed tailplane tab
105 Static discharger
106 Port all-moving tailplane
107 Afterburner nozzle control jacks (6)
108 Tailplane pivot bearing
109 Tailplane hydraulic jack
110 Airbrakes (4), upper and lower surfaces
111 Airbrake hydraulic jack
112 Afterburner duct
113 Ventral fin, folded (undercarriage down) position
114 Ventral fin control jack
115 Lower UHF antenna
116 Ventral fin down position
117 Engine accessory equipment bay
118 Wing root seal
119 Port spoilers/lift dumpers
120 Flap guide rails
121 Port plain flap
122 Fixed spoiler strips
123 Static discharger
124 Port navigation light
125 Leading edge flap (lowered)
126 Port wing integral fuel tank
127 Wing pylon mounting rib
128 Extended-chord sawtooth leading edge
129 Port mainwheel
130 Mainwheel door/debris guard
131 Shock absorber strut
132 Hinged axle beam
133 Articulated mainwheel leg strut
134 Hydraulic retraction jack
135 Fuselage stores pylon
136 Twin missile launcher
137 AA-8 'Aphid' short range air-to-air missile
138 GSh-23L twin-barrel 23mm ventral cannon pack
139 Gun gas venting air scoop
140 AA-2 'Atoll' air-to-air missile
141 Fuselage centreline pylon
142 Ventral fuel tank (176Imp gal/800lit capacity)
143 Wing glove pylon
144 Missile launch rail
145 AA-7 'Apex' long range air-to-air missile

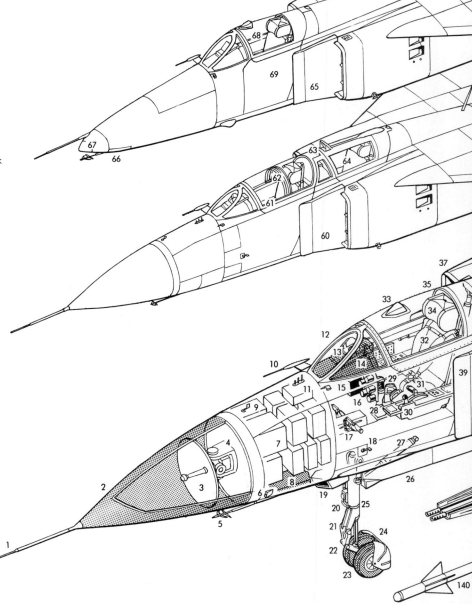

some years; both were probably considered in the development stages. The turbofan is an attractive partner for the VG layout. Without reheat, its specific fuel consumption (SFC) is much better than that of the pure jet, leading to a substantial improvement in range. Because of its large-volume, oxygen-rich exhaust, it can also provide a tremendous thrust boost in reheat, so that its augmented thrust/weight ratio – a key factor in combat performance – is superior to that of the turbojet.

All Western VG aircraft have augmented turbofan powerplants. However, they are all designed for missions that include either long low-level sectors or long loiter times. The engine is in dry thrust nearly all the time, and the lower SFC of the turbofan is critical. That was not the case for a tactical fighter such as the new MiG.

A common factor in nearly all Western augmented turbofans is that their development has been extremely difficult. The most commonly encountered problem is that the augmentor fails to run smoothly in the mixture of hot and cool air fed to it by the engine, and that fluctuations in the augmentor pressure send pulses up the bypass duct and into the fan, which is also the low-pressure compressor. The disturbance thus affects the airflow into the high-pressure compress-

or, causing the engine to suffer from chronic stalls.

Turbofans also run hotter than turbojets. Much of the airflow bypasses the 'core', which comprises the high-pressure compressor, combustor and turbine, but these components provide

Above: India is a major operator of the 'Flogger' family, with three variants in service: the MiG-23BN strike fighter, MiG-23M fighter and the MiG-27M, the last-named being built at Nasik by HAL and bridging the gap between the MiG-21 and MiG-29.

all the engine's power: the fan merely converts it into thrust. They are smaller than the same components in a turbojet of the same thrust, and in order to generate as much power from half as much air, they must have a higher pressure ratio. This is one of the reasons why turbofans are more efficient than turbojets. However, increasing temperatures go hand in hand with higher pressures, and temperatures in the hottest part of the engine – just downstream of the combustor, and ahead of the turbine – are much higher in a turbofan.

Supersonic complications

In a supersonic aircraft, the problem is compounded. At high speeds, the inlet compresses and heats the incoming air, and the temperature at the compressor face rises rapidly with increasing speed. This temperature increase is then multiplied by the pressure ratio of the engine. The result is that supersonic turbofans must run at turbine entry temperatures (TET) some 600°F (330°C) higher than a

Below: Rugged simplicity of construction is a hallmark of the MiG-23 design. Note in particular the robust forgings which form the heart of the design. Also, large access panels are almost absent; these are not required by Soviet maintenance philosophy.

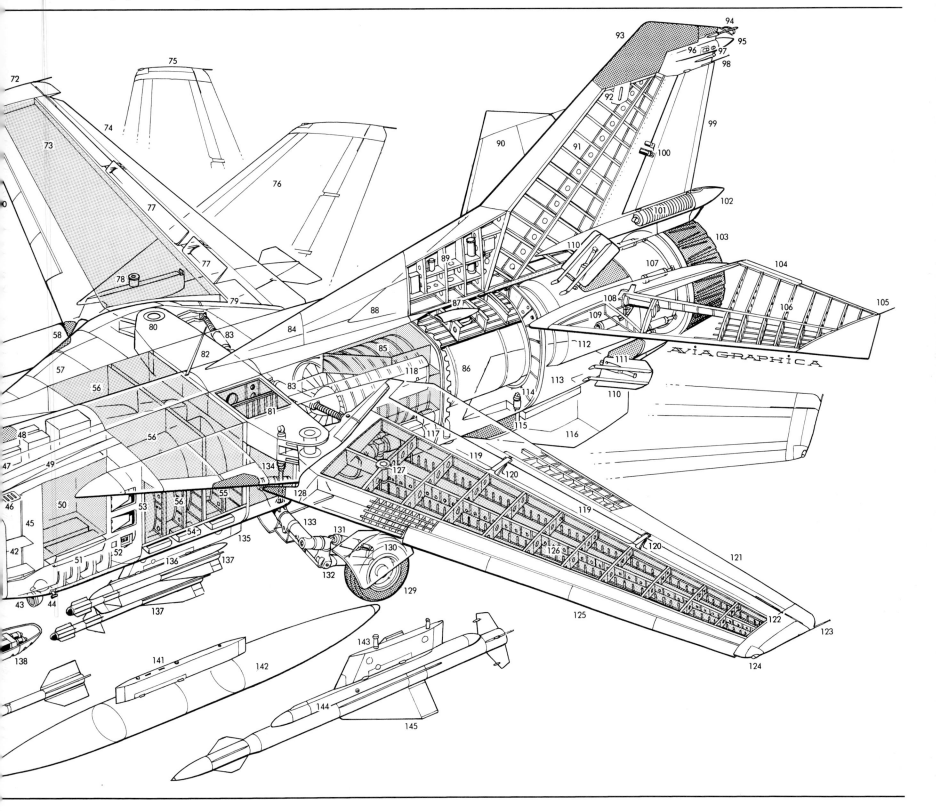

turbojet at the same speed. Turbine life has been the other main problem in the development of supersonic augmented turbofans.

High temperatures and pressures have another effect on the engine. Increasing heat calls for different, more exotic materials and more sophisticated cooling techniques, while higher pressures demand closer tolerances in manufacture and maintenance. The result is that a turbofan is inevitably more expensive than a turbojet, by a considerable margin.

Considering the potential difficulties and costs of the turbofan against its performance advantage, the Soviets decided to stay with the turbojet. (Such a decision would probably be taken by MAP, with inputs from the engine and airframe OKBs and the production organization, and would be approved by the MoD.) Published and apparently reliable data for the Tumansky powerplant, which was designated R-27, overwhelmingly fall into line with values for a turbojet.

Like the Tumansky engines developed for the MiG-21, the R-27 was a two-shaft powerplant with little if any variable geometry. Its pressure ratio was similar to that of Western turbojets such as the J75 and J79, but, being a decade later in design, it used more advanced aerodynamics to achieve a greater pressure rise in each stage, so the number of stages was smaller (eleven in all, compared with 15 for the J75 and 17 for the J79). The engine was accordingly shorter and lighter, developing 25 per cent more thrust than the later models of the J79 but weighing about the same as the older engine.

The Tumansky engine had a similar mass flow and diameter to the older Lyulka AL-7 turbojet. Later, the R-27

Top: Czech Air Force MiG-23BNs are similar to those supplied to India. Clearly visible on the nearer aircraft is the armour plate – almost certainly titanium – applied to the sides of the cockpit.

Above: Apparent in this view of an Indian Air Force MiG-23BN is the improved downward view provided by the attack fighter's shorter, wedge-shaped nose. The head-up display combiner is also visible.

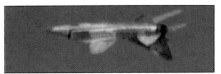

Left: Medium sweep probably gives the best compromise between speed and agility. This sequence shows that the overwing spoilers are used to aid roll control up to fairly high speeds.

would replace the AL-7 in developed versions of the Sukhoi 'Fitter', but this commonality may well have allowed the Mikoyan OKB to use the AL-7 as a reliable and proven substitute for the R-27 during early flight tests of its new fighter prototypes.

Despite its unusual powerplant, the Ye-230 Stol prototype appears to have been completed earlier than the VG aircraft, making its first flight in 1966. The Ye-230 was a handsome design. Aft of the front wing attachments, it was basically a MiG-21, scaled up by about 1.25:1. The wing planform, circular-section fuselage and landing gear geometry were all similar to those of the smaller type. The forward fuselage was entirely new. Ahead of the wing, it widened to accommodate half cone, axisymmetrical side inlets, flanking a compactly designed, oval-section nose containing the cockpit, above the nosewheel well, with avionics racks behind the cockpit and the radar bay and radome in front. A bay in the centre fuselage, between the inlet ducts, accommodated two lift-jets in the 5,500lb (2,500kg) thrust class, probably developed by the Kolesov bureau.

The Ye-231 VG prototype – the entire programme bore the Ye-23 designation, different configurations being identified by three-digit designators – flew in early 1967. Apart from the forward fuselage and nosewheel, which were identical to those of the Ye-230, it was a completely different aircraft, and owed no specific features to any other MiG design. Typically, though, it was logically laid out and full of interesting detail.

The wing itself was slender and quite thin in section, and carried plain, full-span trailing-edge flaps split into three segments, and overwing spoilers for low-speed roll control and lift dumping. The movable outer wings could be moved into three positions – 16°, 45° and 72° – under manual control. There was no provision for movable wing pylons. Sealing around the junctions with the glove and fuselage presented no great problems, because the wing was thin and the apertures were short, and was carried out with small spring-loaded metal panels. The wing incorporated a certain amount of taper and twist, tending to off-load the tips and reduce the shift of the aerodynamic centre. The tailerons had cropped tips in the new standard style, to avoid flutter problems, and were independently actuated to provide high-speed roll control.

Structural features

Structurally, the new type followed MiG-21 practice, with a mix of conventional light alloy and high-strength steel. MAP's production organization continued to display a fondness for massive forging presses, and these were used to make the key bulkheads, the wing carry-through structure and the spars.

The inlets were of the vertical-ramp type, but were based on the design developed by the central propulsion bureau, TsIAM, for the new Sukhoi Su-15. A primary splitter wedge performed the dual function of clearing off the turbulent air close to the fuselage and forming the primary shock wave ahead of the inlet aperture. Hinged to the rear of this plate was a movable ramp, back-to-back with another ramp inside the inlet. The two ramps moved outward to narrow the inlet at high speed, while boundary-layer flow adhering to the inlet ramp was drawn through tiny perforations in the ramp and vented overboard. Simple in

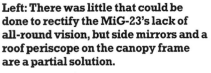

Left: There was little that could be done to rectify the MiG-23's lack of all-round vision, but side mirrors and a roof periscope on the canopy frame are a partial solution.

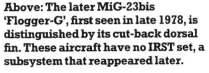

Above: The later MiG-23bis 'Flogger-G', first seen in late 1978, is distinguished by its cut-back dorsal fin. These aircraft have no IRST set, a subsystem that reappeared later.

Below: The MiG-23 cockpit is basically simple and features a large number of single-message caution and warning captions. Critical radar and weapon data is displayed on the HUD.

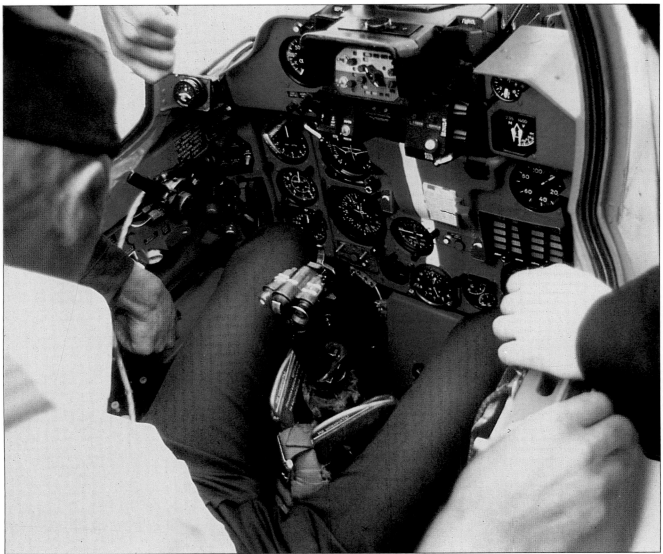

function, these inlets had been shown to work well at speeds up to Mach 2.4 At low speeds, two suck-in auxiliary doors in each inlet wall provided additional airflow.

The main landing gear was unique. Each levered-suspension unit was attached to a massive beam, pivoted close to the aircraft centreline and shaped to fit in the space between the inlet duct and the fuselage side. As the gear retracted, the beam swung upward into the fuselage side, and the wheel folded downward to lie behind and parallel to the beam. While heavy and complex in itself, the gear design took up very little volume in the fuselage and incredibly little of the valuable area on the surface, while clearing both wing and centreline stores and providing a wide track for ground stability. Its only drawback was that it was rather short, giving the aircraft a tail-down, waddling gait and failing to provide more than minimal ground clearance for under-fuselage stores.

Directional stability was clearly an issue, because of the high design speeds and the rearward movement of the aerodynamic centre. The fin was large, and carried a massive dorsal extension which stretched almost half-way along the fuselage. For a further increase in vertical area, with its effect enhanced by the dynamic pressure under the fuselage, the designers incorporated a single very large ventral fin, which folded upward and to the right as the landing gear was extended. Also prominent in the design of the rear fuselage were the four separate airbrake segments, above and below the tailplanes, which provided powerful deceleration without any trim changes.

VG and jet-lift offered different advan-

tages, but it does appear that they were pursued as alternative approaches to the design of a tactical fighter. However, VG proved convincingly superior overall. Even the mid-span-pivot demonstrator, the Sukhoi S-221, was unexpectedly adopted as a production aircraft. The Ye-231 was selected as the basis for the next tactical fighter, but it also served as an aerodynamic technology demonstrator for a new all-weather strike aircraft developed by the Sukhoi bureau. The resulting Su-24 is virtually a 1.2:1 linear scale-up of the Ye-231 planform.

Jet-lift Stol disadvantages

Precisely why jet-lift Stol was abandoned is not known. Obviously, combat radius would be compromised by the loss of internal volume to the vertical propulsion system, but this would be offset to some degree by the ability to take off without using reheat, and the Stol fighter could also operate from shorter strips close to the front. Other disadvantages might be harder to accept. The combination of low flight speeds and a large mass of air passing vertically through the fuselage must have had effects on stability that were interesting, to say the least. Also, any severe pitch-up would have caused simultaneous reduction in lift and a reverse thrust component. Experience from the programme, however, helped development of the Yak-38 shipboard Vtol fighter.

Strategic changes may also have contributed to the ending of the Stol programme. In 1967, NATO had shifted from a strategy of nuclear retaliation to a doctrine of 'flexible response', emphasizing a gradual increase in the commitment of military force and a delayed use of nuclear weapons. Among Soviet doctrinal changes in response was a new emph-

Above: Taken during the same display as the photograph below, this shows the same aircraft turning with medium sweep. At any sweep angle, however, the MiG-23 does not match the manoeuvrability of later fighters.

asis on mobility, and the ability to make rapid and deep advances into enemy territory. The role of tactical air power, too, became more offensive, with the stress on destroying enemy air assets rather than defending and supporting the ground troops. The changes in doctrine were important for the MiG-23. In particular, the FA now needed a 'counter-air' fighter of much greater range than the MiG-21, and it was in this area that the VG aircraft excelled.

The Ye-231 made a brief appearance at the Domodedovo air show in June 1967, and received the NATO code-name 'Flogger'. Thereafter, it disappeared from Western eyes for almost four years. Even its true service designation, MiG-23, was thought to apply to the 'Foxbat'.

Development was not fast, and its course is not entirely clear. Prototype testing is believed to have continued through the rest of the 1960s, until by 1969-70 the future of the programme had been settled: it had been decided to defer large-scale production, pending substantial modifications to the design. Meanwhile, a small batch of service-test aircraft, based on the prototype but carrying some operational equipment,

would be issued to FA units for further evaluation. Designated MiG-23S, and known to NATO, like the prototype, as 'Flogger-A', these aircraft were in service by 1971.

By that time the first true production model was flying. The MiG-23M, later named 'Flogger-B' by NATO, incorporated some major changes. These have been consistently misrepresented by so many authoritative sources that the correct version is seldom heard.

The new version retained virtually all the structure of the prototype. The centre-section wing structure was retained, including the gloves and the pivots, and most of the fuselage was externally similar to the original. The overall fuselage length was unchanged. It is important to

Above: Indian Air Force MiG-23BN climbs out with full afterburner. The variable inlets and fully variable nozzle of this version are of little use in its normal operating regime – high subsonic speed at low level.

note that the fuselage was not shortened, nor were the wing pivots moved forward on the gloves; it is obvious that the latter step would have been geometrically impossible without closing the gap between the pivots, redesigning the carry-through structure and revising the fuselage.

The main external changes were confined to the outer wing panels and the tail surfaces. The outer wing panels were new. While the span and tip chord were

unchanged, a very large leading-edge extension was added to the planform, increasing chord at the root of the moving panel by more than 20 per cent. This extension terminated abruptly in a huge 'claw' outboard of the glove, so that the pivot geometry remained unaltered. The design of the claw was such that it formed a narrow slot at minimum sweep, a streamwise dog-tooth at intermediate sweep, and a streamlined discontinuity with the wings swept aft. The trailing-edge flaps were unchanged, roll-control spoilers were added, and the outer two-thirds of the outer-panel leading edge were made into a simple nose flap.

The tailerons and most of the fin and rudder were structurally unchanged, but

were moved aft by about 24in (61cm). The dorsal fin extension, already large, was further stretched to retain its original starting point on the fuselage. The ventral fin was not moved.

The reason for the changes is not known. The original Ye-231 layout was retained with great success in the Su-24, so it presumably had no fundamental shortcomings. However, the aerodynamic effects of the modifications can be broken down as follows:
☆ Increased wing area and lift coefficient (through the new leading-edge flaps), permitting higher weights at take-off;
☆ Increased taper, reducing the shift of aerodynamic centre with wing-sweep changes;

Left: Wings fully aft and throttle fully forward, a MiG-23bis pulls up during a display in Sweden. The stable pattern of precipitation along the leading edge shows that the notch is doing its job and preventing tip stall.

Right: An Indian Air Force MiG-23BN rolls out after landing. The brake parachute is used routinely, but it is interesting to note that neither spoilers nor airbrakes are deployed.

Below: Landing after its demonstration in Sweden, a MiG-23bis deploys its brake chute. The more level ground attitude of the later version, with its revised landing gear, is notable.

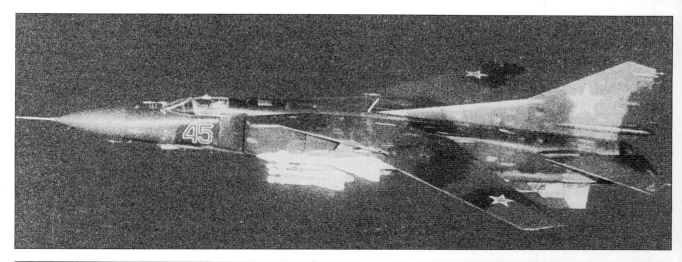

Right: In the early 1980s, MiG-23s were first observed carrying AA-8 'Aphid' short-range AAMs in pairs on the belly pylons. The double row of forward fins can be seen clearly in the missiles carried by this MiG-23M.

☆ Moving the aerodynamic centre forward, and the tail surfaces aft, lengthening the tail 'moment arm' and increasing the effectiveness of the control surfaces;

☆ Moving the aerodynamic centre forward while, if anything, moving the centre of gravity rearward, reducing static stability margins;

☆ Moving the tailerons clear of the wing wake;

☆ Providing a leading-edge break to shed a strong vortex over the wing, inhibiting outward airflow and delaying tip-stall and pitch-up.

It is almost certain that the main aim of the modifications was to make the aircraft more manoeuvrable. The F-111, which has a very similar wing and tail geometry, becomes excessively stable in pitch – that is to say, nose-heavy – as the wings sweep back. The result is a reduction in manoeuvrability and, because a greater amount of control power is required to trim and manoeuvre the aircraft, an increase in drag in both level and manoeuvring flight. By making the configuration less naturally stable and increasing the control authority, the modifications applied to the MiG-23 increased the instantaneous turn rate; lengthening the moment arm also reduced the trim drag, while the vortices shed by the claws would inhibit a complete departure from controlled flight, which might be made more likely by the reduced stability margin. The Su-24, which does not need improved manoeuvrability, retains the original TsAGI shape.

Apart from these major changes, there were relatively few modifications other than those connected with operational equipment. One was the introduction of horizontal vanes into the inlet, behind the variable ramp, a simple but effective way of curbing unruly airflows at high angles of attack. The clean shape was disrupted by some semi-external conduits, but the fuselage remained basically unaltered.

MiG-23M operational equipment

The new MiG-23M was a fully operational aircraft, with a full range of equipment. The nose was occupied by the fire-control radar; its Soviet designation is unknown, but it is codenamed 'High Lark' by NATO. It is a J-band radar working on the pulse-Doppler principle, with circuitry that analyzes the Doppler shift in return echoes. Emissions from the original 'High Lark', recorded by Western electronic intelligence assets, were considered to be suspiciously similar to those of the Westinghouse AWG-10 fitted to the F-4J Phantom; some F-4Js had been lost over Vietnam in 1967-68, and it has been suggested that the original 'High Lark' owes a great deal to recovered AWG-10 specimens. In any event, the 'High Lark' was a respectable performer for its time, with some ability to detect low-flying targets against ground clutter. (This 'look-down' capability must be distinguished from 'look-down, shoot-down'; 'High Lark' cannot guide a missile on to a low-flying target.)

In consideration of the changes in the fighter mission, and the possibility that the new fighter might operate beyond the range of ground control, the MiG-23 became the first Soviet fighter to feature a long-range navigation system, in the form of Doppler. Beneath the nose of the MiG-23M was a prominent housing with an optically flat glass front. This is gener-

Above: Illustrating the Soviet Union's confidence in its allies is this export-model 'Flogger-E' of the Libyan AF, with the radar/missile system of the MiG-21MF. One Libyan MiG-23 pilot crashed in Italy, probably while trying to defect.

Right: A SovAF MiG-23bis. In sharp contrast to the aircraft above, it has an incomparably better radar, IRST set (not the same as that of the MiG-23M), missiles of a later generation, more power and provision for much more fuel. Released in 1985, this is the first shot of a MiG-23bis with three tanks.

ally considered to house an infra-red search and tracking device, for passive target tracking and positive identification.

Other antennas, built into the nose, the tailfin tip, the gloves and the tips of the claws, betrayed the presence of defensive and communications systems. The large dielectric panel at the tip of the fin housed the datalink antenna; a rear-facing bullet on the fin, and forward-facing antennas on the wings, probably housed the Sirena radar-warning receiver (RWR) system. The three differently shaped vertical aerials of the 'Odd Rods' IFF system spout ahead of the windshield, and bow-and-arrow antennas, reported to be part of the 'Swift Rod' instrument landing system, are carried on the nose and fin. In the lower rear fuselage is an array of 20 small holes; their purpose is not known for certain, but they may well be dispensers for flares and chaff cartridges, used as last-ditch missile decoys.

From the outset, the MiG-23 was designed to carry an internal GSh-23 cannon. (Interestingly, the Ye-230 had appeared at Domodedovo in 1967 with an accurate mock-up of the gun pack, before the weapon itself was known in the West.) The installation was similar to that of the MiG-21PFMA and subsequent variants, as discussed in the previous chapter.

The primary armament of the new fighter was to comprise the new R-23 and R-60 missiles, respectively designed for long-range interception and dogfighting. The R-23 was a new departure for the Soviet Union, being the first Soviet weapon intended for BVR attacks on small targets; known to NATO as AA-7 'Apex', its most striking characteristic is its size. It is about 20 per cent longer than its closest Western equivalent, the Sparrow, and its body diameter is 30 per cent larger. Taken together, these figures suggest that the R-23 weighs some 950lb (430kg), or about twice as much as the Sparrow. However, its effective range is no greater than the Sparrow's.

R-23 design rationale

These characteristics, unimpressive on paper, probably reflect a conservatism that was justified at the time. In Vietnam, the only theatre where BVR missiles had been used, the results had not been good, with kill probability (PK) figures in the 0.1-0.2 range: one shot in five or ten would be successful. The answer was either to improve the technology – which the Soviet Union could not count on doing, because this was a first-generation fighter-versus-fighter weapon – or to be more conservative in

what was expected of each part of the system. The key was probably to trade greater weight for an acceptable PK. Whether this was accomplished successfully is hard to assess, since the R-23 has never been used in action.

The layout of the R-23, with foreplanes, delta wings and tailfins, suggests a concern with providing enough aerodynamic manoeuvrability to pursue a target through an evasive manoeuvre: Vietnam had shown the difficulty of achieving surprise with a missile shot, because of radar signals and the missile's thick exhaust plume. In addition, the R-23 may have a larger fraction of its weight devoted to the warhead, and to multiple fuzing systems to ensure that it detonates.

In common with Soviet interceptor-borne missiles, the R-23 is carried in two versions, one with infra-red homing and one with semi-active radar homing. The missiles can be released separately or in sequence, complicating the opponent's countermeasures problem and increasing the chances of a hit. One advantage of the TsAGI VG configuration is that it provides space below the gloves for the substantial pylon which this weapon requires.

MiG-23 stores options

1 Tactical air-to-surface missiles
2 AA-8 'Aphid' (R60) air-to-air missiles
3 GP-9 pack (23mm GSh-23 and ammunition)
4 176Imp gal (800lit) centreline fuel tank
5 AA-2 'Atoll' IR-homing air-to-air missile

High speed and a heavy armament are the MiG-23's strong points. While AAMs are the primary armament, anti-radiation missiles and other air-to-surface weapons not requiring specific guidance systems can also be carried.

MiG-23 combat avionics

1 'High Lark' radar
2 Main avionics compartments
3 Sirena 3 radar warning receiver
4 VHF antenna
5 HF notch
6 VHF/UHF antenna
7 'Swift Rod' ILS antenna
8 VHF omnidirectional range antenna
9 Not known
10 Laser ranger and marked target seeker

MiG-23 stores provision

1 GSh-23 with 200rds ammunition
2 Centreline pylon for 176 Imp gal (800lit) fuel tank
3 Fuselage pylon, capacity 1,650/2,200lb (750/1,000kg)
4 Wing glove pylon, capacity 2,200lb (1,000kg)

The other missile developed for the MiG-23 was the R-60. This, by contrast, is the smallest of all fighter-launched guided weapons. With its relatively large delta wings and its double nose fins, it is clearly designed for high agility, so that it can turn rapidly from its launch path on to the target and confound any evasive manoeuvre. This should give it a small minimum range, and the ability to engage any target of sufficient brightness within the range of its seeker head. The forward nose fins are fixed, and may act as 'slats' for the aft set of fins, turning the airflow towards them and delaying a stall at very high g. The R-60, known to NATO as AA-8 'Aphid', is also used in semi-active radar and IR versions, the former being used for front-aspect attacks.

Missile deployment
Production of the MiG-23 seems to have run ahead of the development of the new missiles. When the type was first observed in East Germany, in the course of 1973, it was seen to be carrying launch rails for K-13-type missiles. The new weapons probably entered service in the Soviet Union in the mid-1970s, and were kept away from the less secure areas of Eastern Europe and the Baltic until the early 1980s. Initially, the glove pylons each carried a single R-23, and the belly pylons each mounted one R-60; dual launchers for the R-60 or K-13-class weapons have been seen on the glove pylons, replacing the R-23 rail; also, twin R-60 rails can be fitted to the belly pylons. While the MiG-23 can in theory carry eight short-range missiles, two R-23s and four R-60s seem to constitute the normal armament.

A routine and parallel development was the production of a two-seat conversion trainer variant, the MiG-23U. The second cockpit, with poor natural visibility ameliorated by a retractable periscope, displaced some of the fuel and avionics. Part of the latter was relocated to the nose, and the smaller 'Jay Bird' radar replaced the 'High Lark' system to make room for it.

The MiG-23 was fast, heavily armed, and had a respectable range, but NATO

Above: One of a batch of photos taken at Tripoli in 1975, which revealed the existence of the 'export' MiG-23.

Right: Points of interest in this nose-to-nose confrontation between MiG-23BN and Jaguar at an Indian Air Force base include the similarity of the forward fuselage design, the much larger inlets (and greater power) of the MiG, and the Soviet type's short, stout landing gear.

observers were not, to begin with, very disturbed by its arrival. It was clearly not in the class of the new US fighters then under development, and was generally more comparable with the F-4. As 1973 gave way to 1974, however, Western economies recoiled under the impact of the oil embargo and subsequent price rise, and defence plans everywhere came under budgetary pressure. Meanwhile, the number of MiG-23s in the field continued to increase at an ever faster rate, and the West started to take notice.

It soon became clear that the MiG-23 was an outstanding achievement in producibility, even by Soviet standards. This did not result from any single breakthrough, but from the fact that ease of production was a priority at all stages of design. The TsAGI VG planform, for example, was designed to be compatible with a simple fuselage and simple inlet design. The strength of the structure primarily relied on a few components of high-tensile steel, reinforcing the straightforward riveted-alloy airframe. The inlet was a proven design that had been demonstrated to perform properly without a complex control system. Tumansky's engine used advanced design in the aerodynamics to reduce the number and cost of the individual stages. This philosophy was carried right through the airframe.

Right: Egypt took delivery of a number of MiG-23 export models – fighters and MiG-23BNs – before its rift with the Soviet Union. Some of the aircraft seen here may still be in service, at a well concealed airfield on Nellis AFB, Nevada.

Above: Indian Air Force MiG-23BNs of the first production batch delivered from the Soviet Union. HAL is now building the more capable MiG-27M, and MiG-23M fighters have been delivered direct from the Soviet Union.

By the end of 1973, MiG-23 production was probably running at 150 aircraft a year. While the MiG-21 still offered superior manoeuvrability, and would be retained for the tactical air defence mission, the newer fighter was far superior to the MiG-21 and Su-7 in any role that involved long range or an appreciable warload. With sizable fleets of such obsolescent types in being, the opportunity to carry out a rapid replacement programme, and to reply firmly to NATO's flexible response strategy, could not be missed. It was decided to accelerate production of the MiG-23 to unprecedented levels.

The factors behind individual Soviet planning decisions are kept secret. It is no secret, however, that Soviet industry's forte is the production of mechanical devices: airframes, engines, tanks and the like. In the case of almost any weapon system, it is found that the production of electronics and electronics-based subsystems lags behind that of the platform itself. In the case of the MiG-23M, the most likely components to present such a problem would be the 'High Lark' radar and the new missiles.

In the case of a Western aircraft in the same position, production would probably not be started until the radar production rate could match that of the airframe. The Soviet front commander, though, would rather have the faster, more powerful aircraft as soon as possible. It is possible that considerations of this sort underlay the development of new versions of the MiG-23, the first of which appeared quite suddenly on the scene in mid-1975.

Left: MiG-23BNs of the IAF's No 10 'Winged Dagger' Squadron. All these aircraft feature a small dielectric cap on a fairing above the starboard glove pylon; however, this is not always present on IAF aircraft of the type.

The simplest adaptation, and possibly the first to be developed, was basically a MiG-23M with the 'High Lark' radar, IR system and missile-control electronics removed, and replaced by a version of the MiG-21's 'Jay Bird' radar. Armament comprised four K-13-class missiles. It was this version that was supplied to Syria, Iraq and Libya in 1974-75. However, it has also been seen in Soviet markings.

A more extensively modified aircraft was developed to supersede some of the many Su-7s, MiG-21s and older MiGs in the tactical strike role. The first step in this line of development was a basic MiG-23 up to the rear cockpit bulkhead, but with a completely new forward fuselage which was shorter, lighter, cheaper to manufacture and offered a better downward view. It also carried armour on the cockpit sides. The new nose had no provision for a large attack radar, but contained a laser rangefinder. This version was designated MiG-23BN.

Strike variant

At the same time, a more extensive revision of the design was carried out, to produce an optimized strike aircraft. To reduce empty weight, at the cost of operationally useless Mach 2+ capability, the new type was fitted with simple fixed inlets and a shorter, lighter nozzle, while its payload was increased through a number of modifications. To increase the under-fuselage capacity, the fuselage weapon pylons were moved from the underside of the fuselage proper to the inlet ducts, making it possible to carry larger stores; new landing gear support beams increased ground clearance so that a large store or a drop tank could be carried on the centreline; and a small rack was added on each side of the rear fuselage These racks are usually described as mountings for auxiliary take-off rockets, but in fact carry additional stores, or flare or chaff dispensers.

For long-range missions, non-swivelling hardpoints were provided for two more 175gal (800lit) fuel tanks under the wings; the tanks would be used at the start of the flight, and jettisoned before the wings were swept. The wheels and

Mikoyan MiG-27 'Flogger-D'

The MiG-27 is a fully developed, extended-range strike version of the family. Excess weight – including the variable inlets and nozzle – is removed and replaced by extra fuel, more weapons and additional avionics. Virtually all the aircraft of this type have been delivered to Soviet units.

brakes were enlarged to handle the higher gross weight of the new type, and were covered by bulged doors. Almost certainly, the new type introduced the Tumansky R-29 engine, uprated by 15 per cent over the R-27.

Another important change was the provision of a new gun, a six-barrel Gatling-type weapon of 23mm calibre. Not only did this offer a higher firing rate than the GSh-23 – probably in the region of 4,000-5,000 rds/min – but it also had a more sensible 70-calibre barrel length. An unusual – in fact, unique – feature of the installation was that the gun was un-covered, its workings completely ex-posed to the elements. This suggests that the gun is free to move in elevation, a technology that the Soviet Union is known to have exploited in later systems.

Gun performance
The rationale behind such a weapon is simple. A shell drops after it is fired, and the distance it drops below the barrel datum line varies with the firing range. When a fast-moving aircraft is shooting at a much slower ground target, both the range and the ballistic drop change rapidly during the burst. The later shells cover less distance and drop less, so the strikes tend to form an elliptical pattern

Above: Apparent in this view of a MiG-27 are the repositioned pylons, bulged wheel bays and taller main landing gear.

Right: An excellent view of a MiG-27. Note the electro-optical and electronic installations above the glove pylons, nose laser rangefinder, ventral six-barrel Gatling gun, 'scabbed-on' cockpit armour and rear-fuselage stores pylons.

with its long axis on the flightpath. Now, if the gun is trainable, and controlled by an automatic system with access to accu-rate range data (from a laser range-finder) and accurate groundspeed data (from Doppler), the barrel can be steadi-ly depressed during the burst, compen-sating for the shorter range and closing up the hit pattern. Even a simpler sys-tem, based on airspeed or a pre-set de-pression rate, could reduce the shell dis-persion and increase the number of hits.

The improved ground-attack aircraft also featured a further outbreak of avionics: upgraded Doppler beneath the forward fuselage, an unidentified dielec-tric panel, possibly for a terrain-avoidance radar, under the nose, and two small dielectric bulges on the sides

of the nose. The most significant addi-tions, though, were installed on the gloves, directly above the pylons: an electronic antenna to starboard and an electro-optical head to port.

These were directly connected with the new air-to-surface guided weapons under development in the Soviet Union. Even in 1985, very little is known about these weapons. The only one to have been carried outside Soviet airspace is the AS-7 'Kerry', a radio-command guided weapon in the same class as the obsolete US Bullpup. More advanced weapons include the AS-10, a semi-active, laser-guided weapon, the heavier laser-guided AS-14 and the anti-radar AS-12. There is also a 1,100lb (500kg) laser-guided bomb. Seven new

ASMs have been deployed since the mid-1970s, according to the DoD.

Increased payload, structural changes and, above all, provision for stand-off ASMs made the new variant a very diffe-rent machine from the fighter versions, or the original strike aircraft. Accord-ingly, it received the designation MiG-27. Its arrival in East Germany, in mid-1975, came as a total and unpleasant surprise to NATO; even worse, the 16th Air Army had four regiments of this highly effec-tive strike aircraft by the end of the year. It was a quantum jump in capability over the Su-7, and its appearance threatened to end NATO's large margin of qualita-tive superiority over the Warsaw Pact.

Some, but by no means all, of the im-provements incorporated in the MiG-27

Left: This was the first photo of a 'duck-billed' MiG-23 to be seen in the West. It is a hybrid, with MiG-23 inlets and the MiG-27's duct-mounted pylons, and is almost certainly a development aircraft.

have the same small nose antenna fairings as the MiG-27; these may be command antennas for the AS-7, or part of another earlier-technology ASM system. Some Soviet units also operate this type.

The MiG-23BN served a multiple purpose. Despite its simplified systems, it is an effective 'bomb truck', and is easier and cheaper to produce than the more complex MiG-27. The retention of variable inlets seems paradoxical, but it does mean that the same basic airframe can be changed to a fighter configuration at the final assembly stage if national needs require it.

The new variants were identified by NATO in order of observation; the MiG-23U trainer was 'Flogger-C'; the MiG-27, 'Flogger-D'; the 'export model' MiG-23, 'Flogger-E'; and the MiG-23BN became 'Flogger-F' for Middle East and other export customers, and 'Flogger-H' in its WarPac version.

With the introduction of the MiG-27, a second State Aircraft Factory was brought into the programme, and production surged ahead. By the late 1970s, the Soviet Union was estimated to be building more than 500 MiG-23s and MiG-27s per year. The type was exported throughout the Middle East, to Cuba and to Vietnam, and production of the MiG-27M was licenced to HAL in India, deliveries starting in 1979. The MiG-23S was supplied not only to Frontal Aviation, but also to the PVO, providing some measure of capability against low-flying aircraft and replacing many obsolescent types.

It should be remembered, though, that not all of the aircraft delivered were of the top-grade types. Neither the MiG-23M nor the MiG-27 was confirmed to be in use outside Soviet units – with the exception of the East German Luftstreit-kraefte (LSK), which is under full-time

were applied to the MiG-23BN, which became the export-model ground-attack variant of the family. Something of a mongrel, it had the Mach 2.3 propulsion system of the original MiG-23, but with no search radar it was virtually useless in the high-altitude air-to-air regime. Most of the advanced avionics appear to be missing, including those connected with advanced ASMs, the structure is similar to that of the MiG-23 and the less effective GSh-23 gun is retained. MiG-23BNs delivered to Warsaw Pact air forces

Left: The MiG-27 HUD is similar to that of the MiG-23. The canopy has no central frame; this may mean that the ejection seat is designed to break through the transparency.

Left: The MiG-23BN is another 'export model' which in fact is extensively used by the Soviet Union's own forces; recently, it has been more widely illustrated than the MiG-27, but the latter is probably more important.

AF fighters all had datalinks, and could receive information as it was gathered: the Syrians' own Soviet-supplied datalinks had been effectively jammed by the IDF.

Details of individual actions are hard to come by. However, published figures have suggested that the MiG-23 is outturned by both the MiG-21 and the F-4E, and is in a different class of manoeuvring performance from new generation fighters such as the F-16. In fact, its performance has been compared to that of the F-104: very fast in a straight line, but very slow in a turn. Its assets, however, include a long range, thanks to low overall drag, respectable internal fuel capacity and VG: the operational combat radius of the three-tank 'Flogger-G' has been stated at 600nm (1,100km) by USAF intelligence sources.

'High Lark' performance

The MiG-23 also has a greater radar detection range, and a greater missile range, than some Western types. According to figures supplied by the US Air Force to *Aviation Week* in early 1981, 'High Lark' can detect a fighter-sized target at 42-45nm (78-83km) at 20,000ft (6,100m) and Mach 0.9. At the same altitude, the maximum range for a radar-guided AA-7 launch is 14nm (26km). This is slightly better than the engagement range for the F-4E/AIM-7E combination, but not by a significant amount; worse than the performance of the F-15/AIM-7F; and considerably better than the performance of the F-16/AIM-9 combination. The 'first-look, first-shot' advantage which the MiG-23 enjoys over the F-16 is a major problem for NATO, and will remain so until the long-delayed introduction of the Hughes AIM-120 Amraam.

MiG-23/27 production was scaled down in the early 1980s; probably, one of the plants involved was converted to production of a new design such as the MiG-29. However, the effect of its contribution to the rapid modernization of Soviet and allied units in the 1970s will be felt for a long time. Apart from the F-16, no comparable Western type has proved to be anything like as affordable, and no similarly affordable type can be considered comparable. The MiG-23 and MiG-27 may not be the newest technology, but they will not become obsolete in this decade, and they provide the Warsaw Pact with a firm numerical foundation for its latest modernization efforts.

Soviet command – until the early 1980s, when India and Syria acquired the MiG-23M. Soviet units operate some 2,100 fighter versions of the series, and over 700 strike types. Some of these are of the subtypes usually described as 'export models'. In recent statements of fighter doctrine, for example, it has been made clear that only one aircraft in each fighting pair need be equipped for BVR.

Analysis of the destruction of a Korean Air Lines 747 in September 1983 has suggested that it was intercepted by a pair of aircraft: a BVR-equipped Su-15 and a MiG-23, probably a 'Flogger-E'. The 'Flogger-E' and MiG-23BN are probably in the minority overall, but may predominate in the Southern and Far Eastern theatres. Even if 75 per cent of the Soviet fleet consists of the full-capability variants, it is quite possible that downgraded versions have accounted for half the production run.

'Flogger-G' and 'Flogger-J'

Development continued through the later 1970s. An improved fighter version was first seen in late 1978 when a squadron of the type paid a visit to Finland. Believed to be designated MiG-23bis, the type incorporated a number of changes. The most obvious was a shorter, smaller dorsal fin extension, the precise reason for which is not clear. The type also featured a redesigned landing gear. The new nosewheel leg carried larger tyres, like those of the MiG-27, and the doors were bulged to accommodate it; the mainwheel legs were like those of the MiG-27, providing ground clearance for a 175gal (800lit) tank on the centreline. Like the MiG-27, too, the MiG-23bis can carry underwing tanks of the same capacity on fixed-sweep, jettisonable pylons. Compared with the original fighter version, its fuel capacity is increased by 525gal (2,400lit), or the equivalent of a MiG-21's internal fuel load.

The 'High Lark' radar has been improved, with more 'look-down' capability against low-flying targets (although it cannot guide AA-7 missiles on to them), and the cockpit instrumentation appears to have been modified; the Soviet fighter's usual head-down radar scope has been eliminated, and data is presented instead on the head-up display. This version is known to NATO as 'Flogger-G'.

The most recent version of the family to be identified is a MiG-27 variant known as 'Flogger-J' and featuring a

slightly different nose profile. The EO and RF heads above the glove pylons have been deleted, and the pylons often carry gun pods with depressable barrels. Some 'Flogger-J' aircraft have been seen with narrow leading-edge root extensions; these seem too small to have much of an effect on the turn rate, and may house antennas.

MiG-23 exports started just after the Arab-Israeli war of 1973. It was an unlikely harbinger of peace, but it was to be eight years before the type was used in action. In June 1982, the MiG-23 made its combat debut, and emerged on the wrong side in the greatest military disaster in the history of air warfare.

Following Israel's invasion of Lebanon, Syria moved to install SAMs in the Beka'a Valley. The Israel Defence Force-Air Force (IDF-AF) moved to destroy the missiles and the advancing Syrian troops, and MiG-21s and MiG-23s were deployed to protect them. The combat zone was only two minutes from Syrian bases, while the IDF-AF aircraft had to fly between 10 and 40 minutes to reach the combat zone. The IDF-AF was also under a self-imposed prohibition against entering Syrian airspace.

Within one week, the IDF-AF had destroyed more than 80 Syrian aircraft, including 36 MiG-23s; its own losses did not exceed two aircraft. The general verdict, however, was not that the aircraft itself was totally inferior, since there were many factors in the Israeli success. The IDF-AF certainly displayed better tactics, and the Syrian tactics were judged less effective than they had been in 1973. The IDF-AF also had the advantage of better missile armament, with the

Right: Another photo showing the extensive range of sensors carried by the MiG-27. The four-bomb armament carried here is probably little more than a practice load.

Above: Published here for the first time, this shows a MiG-27 carrying a very large (length 13.5ft/4m) ASM. Bigger than the AS-7 'Kerry', it may be the semi-active laser-guided AS-14, or the anti-radiation AS-9. The pod under the fuselage resembles the underwing gunpods of the 'Flogger-J'.

developed Shafrir and the all-aspect AIM-9L. (According to the IDF-AF, Syria's MiG-23s were armed with R-23s and R-60s.)

Possibly the most important single factor, though, was the highly developed Israeli battle management system, including E-2C Hawkeyes and a fleet of electronic intelligence (elint) platforms ranging from balloons, through OV-1 Mohawks and modified RF-4Es to specially equipped RC-707s. The Syrian fighters were tracked as soon as they left their runways, and the IDF-AF usually had the advantage of surprise. The IDF-

MiG-27 stores options

1 FAB-250 550lb (250kg) general-purpose bomb
2 FAB-500 1,100lb (500kg) general-purpose bomb
3 Tactical air-to-surface missile
4 AA-2-2 'Advanced Atoll' air-to-air missile
5 23mm Gatling gun and ammunition
6 1,100lb (500kg) low-drag bomb
7 176Imp gal (800lit) centreline fuel tank

The most heavily armed member of the series, the MiG-27 can carry and launch most of the new tactical ASMs and smart weapons introduced by Soviet forces over the past ten years.

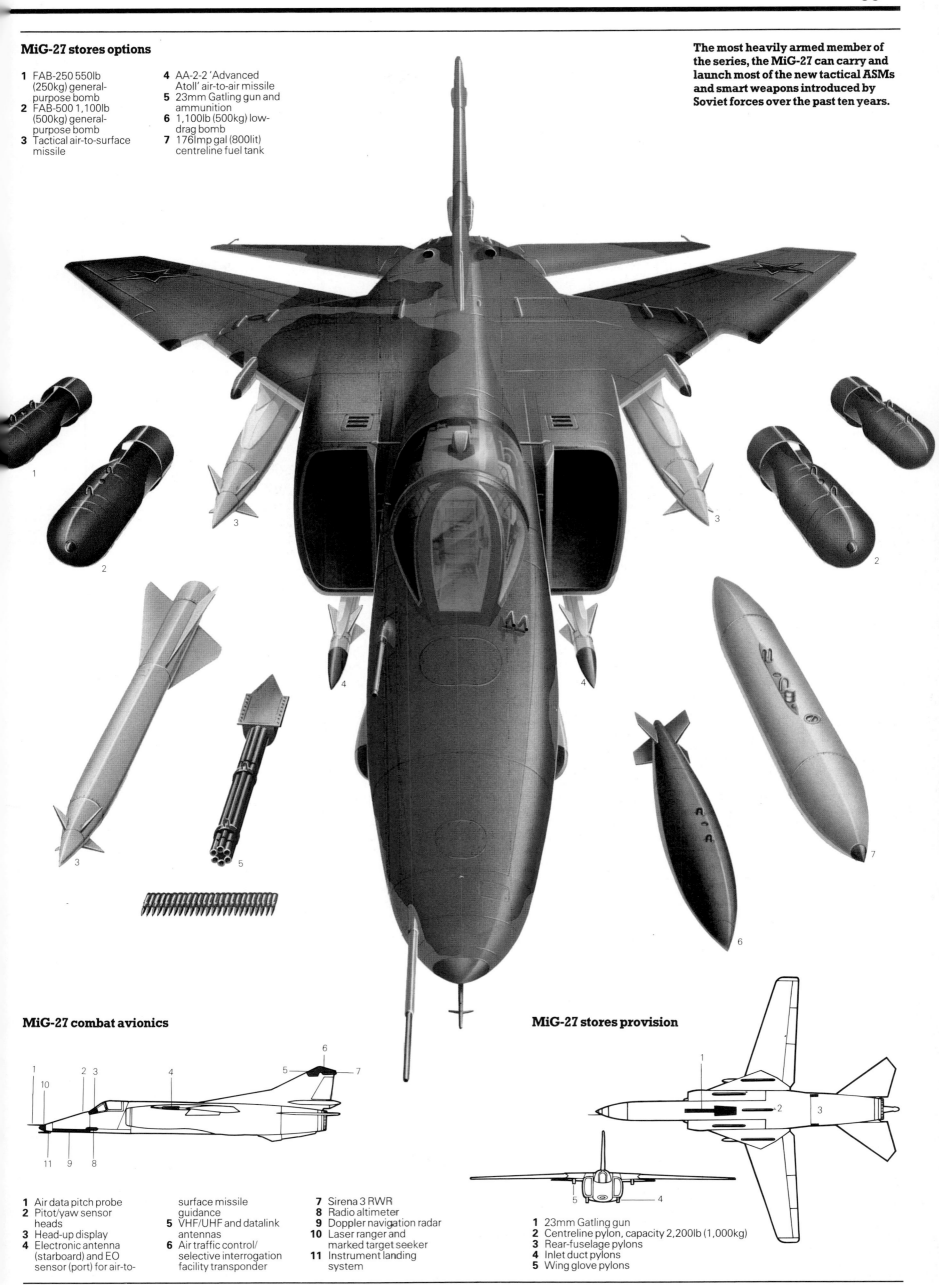

MiG-27 combat avionics

MiG-27 stores provision

1 Air data pitch probe
2 Pitot/yaw sensor heads
3 Head-up display
4 Electronic antenna (starboard) and EO sensor (port) for air-to-
surface missile guidance
5 VHF/UHF and datalink antennas
6 Air traffic control/ selective interrogation facility transponder
7 Sirena 3 RWR
8 Radio altimeter
9 Doppler navigation radar
10 Laser ranger and marked target seeker
11 Instrument landing system

1 23mm Gatling gun
2 Centreline pylon, capacity 2,200lb (1,000kg)
3 Rear-fuselage pylons
4 Inlet duct pylons
5 Wing glove pylons

MiG-25 'Foxbat'

Solid and aggressive in appearance, and uniquely fast in level flight and climb, the MiG-25 has inspired respect since its first appearance. Initially developed as a counter to the cancelled B-70 Valkyrie, the new interceptor was consistently mis-assessed by Western intelligence, with results that permanently affected Western planning. The US Air Force, in particular, incurred enormous expense in developing the F-15 as a counter to what proved to be a mythical aircraft. And the West's errors would probably still stand uncorrected had it not been for a once-in-a-lifetime intelligence windfall in the mid-1970s.

Aviation history is full of surprises. One of the biggest was probably inflicted on the personnel of Hakodate Airport, in northern Japan, one overcast September afternoon in 1976. At 13.50, just as the daily All Nippon Airways 727 lifted off the 6,000ft (1,830m) runway, a jagged steel-grey shape dropped from the clouds, dead in its path. A collision was averted at the last second as the intruder's pilot turned sharply around the 727 and dived for the runway. The aircraft was still moving at 220kt (405km/h) as it touched down, and following a tyre-scorching, parachute-streaming gallop down the length of the remaining concrete it came safely to rest 800ft (243m) into the overrun zone. The airport people stared with slowly diminishing disbelief at the new arrival, the unmistakable red stars of the Soviet Air Forces vivid against its dull skin. Lt Viktor Belenko had defected to the West with his own aircraft, a Mikoyan MiG-25 'Foxbat-A'.

It was as though the paleontological community had discovered a live Tyrannosaurus rex in some South American jungle. Many aerospace professionals heard the news over breakfast in their hotels in London or the English countryside, because the Farnborough Air Show was on. The news had reached Washington in the middle of the night, but the best men of the USAF's Foreign Technology Division were leaving Wright-Patterson AFB before dawn aboard a pair of VC-135s.

The MiG-25 was the most feared and least known of all Soviet aircraft. It was considered to be almost as fast as the Lockheed SR-71, but it had already been built in far greater numbers and was still in production. According to some assessments, its unrefuelled range was comparable to the SR-71's, allowing it to escort Backfire bombers over the North Atlantic or reconnoitre the whole of Western Europe; even the less flattering estimates credited it with range at least equal to that of the new McDonnell Douglas F-15. The MiG-25 had thumbed its nose at Israel's formidable air force. What nobody could understand was how the Soviet designers had packed so much performance into an aircraft that could be built in such numbers.

A myth exposed

The Foreign Technology Division, and the intelligence community in general, were next in line for a surprise. Examination of the aircraft – before it was returned, in pieces, to the Soviet Union – and Belenko's own extensive debriefing, showed that the West had grossly misassessed the MiG-25 from the day of its first public appearance nine years earlier. For almost a decade, a great deal of Western defence planning had been influenced by a mythical aircraft.

The story had started just about two decades earlier, when the US National Advisory Committee on Aeronautics (NACA) published the results of some theoretical work in high-Mach aerodynamics. The theory put forward by Alfred Eggers and Clarence Syvertson was that a supersonic aircraft could be designed to trap its own shock wave beneath its wings, turning otherwise wasted energy into useful lift.

The 'compression lift' theory went unnoticed until January 1957. At that time, Strategic Air Command was looking for a supersonic replacement for the B-52, but the target performance was proving hard to attain, except with an enormous aircraft which, in effect, was 'staged' like a rocket; much of its structure would contain only fuel, and would be jettisoned as the fuel was used. The last few hundred miles to the target would be flown at Mach 2, but cruising speed would be subsonic. Boeing and North American proposed such aircraft to meet the Weapon System 110A (WS-110A) requirement, and both designs were rejected.

In pursuit of an alternative approach, North American turned to the compression-lift theory, and by mid-1957 was proposing a design which was not only more practical, but would fly at Mach 3 throughout its mission, 1,720kt (3185km/h) at an altitude of 70,000ft (21,330m). In December 1957 North America was chosen to build the new bomber, and in the following month SAC cancelled full-scale development of an alternative nuclear-powered bomber in favour of an accelerated schedule for the WS-110A

programme. The new bomber would fly in December 1962, and the first operating wing of 12 aircraft would be operational by August 1964. First details of the programme were released in February 1958, and the designation B-70 was adopted.

To the PVO-Strany, responsible for defending the entire Soviet Union and all its military and industrial centres from bomber attack, the B-70 was a real problem. There were many analysts at the time who would not have agreed with this view. Only months earlier, British officials and Defence Minister Duncan Sandys had rebuilt the country's entire military production programme around the omnipotent guided missile. In the Soviet Union, where amateurs are not encouraged to make policy decisions, a more reasonable view prevailed.

A 200-ton Mach 3 bomber may be an easy target to detect, but it is certainly not easy to kill. Problems start with the mechanics of destroying a large aircraft. Blast is relatively weak in the thin air of high altitude, so a kill requires either a direct hit, by chemical explosives or some heavy kinetic projectile (such as the metal hoop formed by a continuous-rod warhead), or a nuclear blast. Nuclear warheads make the guidance problem less severe, but at the expense of a bigger delivery system.

At the time, the fastest Soviet interceptor was the new Sukoi Su-11. It would not even touch the B-70. Its maximum sus-

Left: A MiG-25R 'Foxbat-B' undergoing flight-line inspection. The sharp waisting of the fuselage between the inlets is very clear in this view, as is the gradual widening of the upper ramps from front to rear.

tained altitude was far lower than that of the B-70, its speed was 30 per cent lower, and its AA-3 'Anab' missiles were designed for use against subsonic bombers.

The Soviet weapon with the greatest capability against high-altitude targets was the new V750VK surface-to-air missile (SAM) system, a large solid-rocket-powered missile with an effective altitude around 75,000ft (22,900m). Despite this, it was a related problem against a B-70, and even a much larger SAM would also suffer certain limitations.

One of these is that a solid-rocket SAM is a 'boost/coast' vehicle: its engines burn out after a few seconds of flight, leaving it with only its momentum. Its ability to turn and manoeuvre is limited by its remaining energy, and beyond a certain point it 'goes ballistic' and will no longer respond to guidance signals. The problem is compounded at high altitudes, where a design conflict arises: the missile's wing size is limited by the need to accelerate rapidly at low altitude, and to keep weight down, but its small wings are inefficient in thin air at higher levels.

On the other hand, the target can manoeuvre: not rapidly, but to an unlimited degree. It also has plenty of warning of an attack, because of the powerful radar signals needed to guide a missile from a ground station. Providing enough of an energy margin to follow an evasive manoeuvre on the part of the target eats further

Above: One of the Ye-26 prototypes takes a bow over Domodedovo on July 9, 1967. Note the vertical fins, much smaller than those adopted for the production MiG-25. The nose is black, but there is probably no radar inside.

er still into the missile's lethal radius.

Speed is a related problem. All missile systems work, to some extent, on prediction, because there is always a time lag between the target's movement and the missile's response: a missile which was guided to the target's actual position would always pass just behind it. With a large command-guided weapon like the V750VK, over a long enough range, the time lag can be quite considerable, and if the target is manoeuvring, and the missile is in its last, sluggish flight phase, the predicted and actual positions of the target may be well apart. Speed also reduces the time available for an engagement, and makes the tracking problem more difficult.

A final point is that the missile is relatively small and expendable, while the aircraft is large, has plenty of onboard power, and is protected by powerful jamming systems. It is probably an accurate generalization to say that jamming gets more effective as the missile approaches the target and flies further from its launch and control system. Because of these and other factors, even a

Right: The MiG-25 'Foxbat-E' has been produced by fitting older airframes with the more effective and less compromised radar of the MiG-23bis, together with a similar IRST system.

Left: Lt Viktor Belenko's MiG-25 rests in the overrun area at Hakodate airport, in northern Japan, following its pilot's defection. It was the largest single windfall of technical intelligence in the superpowers' history.

Below: Although it has a new radar, the 'Foxbat-E' has the same AA-6 missiles as the older aircraft. The appearance of the nose is slightly changed, because the new radome is closer to an ogive than a cone, and is shorter than that of the original.

very large SAM would only have a limited effective radius against an aircraft such as a B-70.

Alternative approaches to a similar problem were being tried in the USA. Because of the 'technology push' mechanism, however, US air defence planning had always been aimed at a projected threat well in advance of anything fielded by the Soviet Union, and by mid-1958 work on an interceptor capable of countering supersonic-cruise bombers was quite well advanced. This was the North American F-108, a large, long-range, two-seat Mach 3 aircraft, equipped with a radar/missile system that could initiate an engagement at 85nm (160km) range. Rather further along in development was the formidable Boeing IM-99 Bomarc, a massive strategic SAM with ramjet propulsion and its own active radar system.

Neither would have worked in the Soviet system. The F-108-type aircraft, with its highly sophisticated electronics, would not have been achievable in time to meet the B-70 threat. In any event, the long-range interceptor was less attractive to the Soviet Union; the land-mass is so large that an adequate multi-layered defensive system can be operated over Soviet territory, where range is not critical, and still protect major targets. As for the Bomarc, the cost of such a large missile, and the chances of actually hitting the target so far from the launch point, were always in doubt.

Instead, the PVO-Strany opted for an extrapolation of the current Soviet interception system. As it stood in 1957-58, the Soviet air defence environment reflected the country's lack of a good radar-equipped interceptor. The IA-PVO – the interceptor component of the force – was divided into a great many small units, usually no larger than a division (three or four regiments of 36 aircraft), each tasked with the defence of a given area or target. The backbone of the force was made up of single-seat interceptors, with limited radar capability.

The fighters were held at readiness on the ground until a target was detected;

they were then scrambled and directed to the interception point by ground controllers. Training and tactics stressed tight control and instant obedience on the part of the pilots, because it was only through close adherence to procedures that a fighter with a low-powered radar could be brought within detection range of its target.

This force structure had some important implications for fighter design. Because the system was originally built around the MiG-15 and MiG-17, each unit's area of operations was restricted to the 160nm (300km) operational radius of those types, and the command and control facilities at unit level were designed to handle the air battle in that area. Now, if a longer-range interceptor were to be introduced, the command and control facilities would have to be expanded to cope with a larger area of operations, and the units' air defence zones would overlap. Without restructuring and re-equipping the ground units, the PVO-Strany simply did not require greater range from its interceptors.

Interceptor performance

Quick reaction, on the other hand, was important, and became more so as the speed of the threat increased. Fighter requirements accordingly stressed speed, rate of climb and reliability. The ability to ensure destruction of the target was also important, and air-to-air missiles received a great deal of attention in the 1950s.

During 1958 the PVO-Strany worked on defining the system needed to intercept the B-70, and what emerged was a requirement for a new single-seat fighter of extremely high performance. It would be designed for a ground-controlled interception (GCI) mission, but the concept would be taken a step further: the fighter would be under automatic control from the ground, and a datalink would connect the fighter's radar to the ground station. The radar would be powerful enough to burn through jamming at close range, providing the ground station with the exact target data needed for the final intercep-

tion. The armament would be a battery of four missiles, each capable of felling a heavy bomber, but with only a modest range; the final attack would be made by the aircraft, not the missiles alone. Maximum speed, with missiles aboard, was to be in excess of 1,620kt (3,000km/h), and the type was to be suitable for mass production.

In speed and range, the new system was not unlike the Bomarc. The main differences were that instead of being expendable, it was recoverable; that it had the ability to make multiple firing passes at the target, increasing its PK; and that it had the added flexibility of a pilot in the loop.

The beauty of this requirement was that, although it stretched the state of the art and was by no means easy, it did not demand any immense advance in any one technology. It avoided the need to develop a long-range radar/missile system, while the modest specified range brought the airframe-design problem within reason. Also, while the datalink would involve new technology, the philosophy of automated GCI meant that many of the complex problems, such as discriminating against jamming and working out the best interception track, could be handled on the ground. Another advantage was that the target would be detected and tracked by ground-based radars; until the final seconds of the interception, when the interceptor turned on its radar, the target's crew need not be aware that they were under attack.

Go-ahead for Mikoyan

The requirement was probably issued in 1959; both Mikoyan and Sukhoi are likely to have been consulted, since both were engaged in developing technology for Mach 2.8 aircraft, but no details of Sukhoi's design, if it existed, are known. In any case, the Mikoyan design was given the go-ahead, probably in early 1960.

In terms of sheer performance, the Mikoyan bureau did not need to aim as high as the Lockheed Skunk Works, which started design of the A-12 reconnaissance aircraft at about the same time,. but were working within far tighter constraints of producibility and reliability. Also, the Soviet system had not encouraged the development of technology for its own sake during the 1950s, and the result was that some of the basic knowledge available to Lockheed was not available to the Mikoyan team.

Even so, building a practical aircraft to carry four heavy missiles and a powerful radar to Mach 2.8 posed problems in many areas. The best known, at the time, was kinetic heating: friction and compression between the air and the airframe generate heat, and above Mach 2 the temperatures begin to reach levels

Above: This was the first photograph released in the West to show the MiG-25 carrying the two-stage AA-6 'Acrid' missile. Semi-active radar-homing weapons are carried on the outer pylons, and IR-homers inboard.

that degrade the structural properties of aluminium, and bring down its fatigue life. The only answer is to substitute a more heat-resistant material.

Aerodynamics also present challenges. As Mach numbers increase, the shock waves shed by the nose and leading-edge surfaces slant back more sharply, and may interact with the rest of the airframe: for instance, the wing leading edge may cut into the nose shock wave, possibly causing excessive drag. Putting the wing completely inside the shock wave either means a very sharply swept wing (with poor low-speed characteristics) or a long and heavy nose; the alternative is a thin-section wing, which is structurally difficult to build. Overall, the design becomes dominated by wave drag.

Stability and controllability

Stability is also an issue. The aerodynamic centre moves rearward at high speeds, so that the aircraft becomes more stable, but it may become excessively stable and more difficult to control. Meanwhile, as Mach number increases, all the aerodynamic surfaces become less affected by changes in angle of attack, and since the tail surfaces stabilize the aircraft by responding to such changes, the dynamic stability of the aircraft decreases. The problem is worse at high altitude, where aerodynamic damping of aircraft movements decreases due to the thinner air. The changes in static and dynamic stability with Mach number make the design and sizing of vertical and horizontal tail surfaces peculiarly critical. The task was particularly difficult in the case of the new interceptor, since it would have to possess some degree of manoeuvrability at its maximum operating speed.

Propulsion for a Mach 3 aircraft is an area for careful trade-off studies. The design of the propulsion system becomes dominated by the ram effect – the high pressure and temperature created when the air entering the inlets at a relative speed of 2,720ft/sec (830m/sec) is slowed down to zero relative speed before entering the engine. This is not quite enough for a ramjet to offer high efficiency, but it creates problems for a conventional turbojet. If the pressure at the compressor face is further multiplied by the engine's own pressure ratio, temperatures within the engine rise to levels where even exotic materials will not be adequate. Also, the design of the inlet system becomes critical, because even a small drop in the amount of ram press-

Above: The fuselage shape of the MiG-25, with the augmentors, forward fuselage and inlet blended into a solid central box, is well depicted in this view of a 'Foxbat-E'. Note also the anti-glare panel ahead of the IRST set.

ure recovered can have a very large effect on efficiency.

Mach 3 flight takes a great deal of power, so the overall efficiency of the propulsion system is important. Even a slight increase in specific fuel consumption translates into a lot of extra fuel. It was this problem that hit the Bristol 188 research aircraft; because the powerplants were not efficient enough, the 188 simply could not carry enough fuel to complete a mission at its design speed.

The fuel system is yet another problem area, for several reasons. High temperatures can detonate empty tanks; heat also causes thermal expansion, making it difficult to seal the tanks properly. On the other hand, as much of the airframe as possible must contain fuel, because of the high thrust requirements.

With these problems in mind, the Mikoyan team threw out all previous designs, along with the normal evolutionary design approach, and started with a clean sheet of paper. The first clear point to emerge, in all probability, was the fact that the new aircraft would be big. The missiles would be large, because of the need for high speed, effectiveness at high altitude and a heavy warhead. The radar system would be heavy, have a large antenna and require a startling amount of power. The resulting rough figures for the size of the aircraft pointed clearly to a twin-engined type, because no single engine would be big enough.

The Mikoyan OKB's trade-off studies on the configuration would make fascinating reading. It is possible to guess that the tailless delta or canard were considered, but probably rejected on the grounds of poor manoeuvrability at high

altitude. The familiar tailed delta was probably ruled out, indirectly, by weight: with fuel for Mach 3 and the required operational equipment, its wing loading would be too high for any high-altitude manoeuvring, and its short span would probably have raised the spectre of inertia coupling.

This left a thin, moderately swept wing as the best practical option. As it happened, the same conclusion had been reached some years earlier by another design team, one which was also aiming for high speed and high altitude, and which also faced requirements that ruled out the otherwise attractive delta wing. Their final design was the highly elegant North American Vigilante, and there can be no question that this very advanced Mach 2 carrier-based bomber, unveiled in 1958, was the starting point for the Mikoyan OKB's design.

Design genealogy

To allocate credit correctly, it must be noted that some key features of the Vigilante configuration stemmed from the Vought F-8 Crusader, flown in 1954, and the first supersonic aircraft to feature a thin swept wing in the structurally convenient shoulder position. The slab tail was set at mid-height on the fuselage, out of the wing wake, another first and a great help to high-speed stability, avoiding the pitch-up problems of a T-tail. At a time when exaggerated 'wasp-waisted' fuselages were the rage, the F-8's clean, straight-lined fuselage demonstrated a clearer understanding of the Area Rule.

The Vigilante inherited these characteristics, adding an advanced propulsion system with variable-geometry, wedge-shaped inlets. The inlet design was more sophisticated than that of the contemporary F-4, and could achieve more efficient ram pressure recovery. The sharp, thrust-forward upper lip split the primary shock past the inlet, but the variable ramps inside the inlet were designed to capture and stabilize the subsequent shock waves. With careful control of bleed valves in the inlet system, this layout was capable of high efficiency across a wide range of flight conditions.

The width of the fuselage and the inlet lips could be a problem at high angles of attack, possibly shedding vortices over the fin. To reduce this effect, the Vigilante designers provided the original design with twin outward-canted vertical fins. These were replaced by a single all-moving slab fin before the prototype was completed.

The twin fins were retained on the new Mikoyan fighter, as were many other aspects of the Vigilante configuration: the thin, shoulder-mounted wing, the inlets, the slab-sided fuselage and the tail position. The detail execution of the design was different, reflecting the different missions, but the two aircraft

turned out to be remarkably similar in shape, size and weight.

The characteristics of the engine, and in particular its thrust and fuel consumption, would determine the size of aircraft needed to meet the mission requirement, while the choice of engine was driven by the timescale and the technical problems. A new turbojet with a normal pressure ratio would have to survive unprecedented operating temperatures, for the reasons discussed above, and development would simply have taken too long. However, there was an alternative available and in production.

During the 1950s, a number of design

Below: The truck by the left-hand MiG-25U carries all the diagnostic equipment for the type, tools for routine maintenance and a ground power unit, and also acts as a tug.

teams had advocated the development of a specialized, simplified 'supersonic turbojet', in which efficiency and low-speed thrust/weight ratio were deliberately sacrificed in the interests of high-speed performance. By 1960, two such engines had been built: the British de Havilland Gyron, and a cruise-missile engine built by the Mikoyan bureau's close associates at the Tumansky OKB. It was this engine that formed the basis for the new interceptor.

The engine's poor low-speed characteristics were of secondary importance, because there was no requirement for subsonic cruise, high-subsonic combat or loiter. However, its appetite for kerosene at Mach 3 would be phenomenal. Studies soon confirmed that the fighter would, indeed, be large, with a loaded takeoff weight of 35-40 tons.

Given the size and the general configuration, the design – now known as the Ye-266 – began to take shape. The size of the wing was set by manoeuvre, climb and sustained altitude requirements, which dictated a maximum wing loading at the top of the climb. (With well over half the fuel gone, this would be much lower than the take-off wing loading.) Sweep angle and thickness/chord ratio were traded off, based on the minimum depth that was structurally practical: a 4 per cent thick wing, swept 40° on the leading edge, was selected, providing low drag but making some room for fuel in the wing. The wing's moderate sweep and low aspect ratio made it stiff enough to accept four pylons for large AAMs, and to allow conventional ailerons to be used for all lateral control. Take-off and landing speed were of secondary importance, and high-lift devices were confined to plain flaps.

The wing was not quite as much of a plank as it appeared. A certain degree of washout – reduction in incidence towards the tips – was introduced by gradually reducing the leading-edge camber from the outer pylon to the tip. At some angles this feature could give a strong impression of compound sweep, and it has confused many observers over the years.

Fuselage design

The shape and size of the engine dictated the build-up of the fuselage. The rear fuselage was wrapped around the huge afterburners, each measuring 49in (1.5m) in diameter. The centre fuselage was a deep, wide box containing the engine tunnels, much smaller in diameter than the augmentors, the simple, forward-retracting main landing gear and much of the fuel. Just ahead of the leading edge, the structure broke into three elements: the two big variable inlets and their ramps, flanking a long nose containing the cockpit and the radar system.

The detailed aerodynamic design of the fuselage was one of its best features. The cross-sectional area was allowed to expand, steadily, from the nose back to the wing. In plan view, the nose section tapered from its maximum width, immediately aft of the radome, to a deep but slender 'neck' between the inlets, reducing total cross-section and avoiding what would otherwise have been a drag-evoking kink in the area-versus-length chart. In fact, the wave drag coefficient of the new design was better than that of the more slender MiG-21 at any speed above Mach 1.5.

The horizontal tail trunnions were angled, as on the MiG-19 and MiG-21, so

Mikoyan MiG-25 'Foxbat-A'

Features of the MiG-25's shape which are frequently overlooked – the straight wing leading edge, the slender 'neck' of the forward fuselage between the inlets, and the tapering inlet lips – are apparent in this old but generally accurate drawing.

that the stabilizers seemed by Western standards to be mounted on little more than thin air. The tips of both the vertical and horizontal surfaces were sawn off at right angles to the quarter-chord line, in what was later recognized as a simple and effective precaution against flutter.

The most original feature of the airframe, though, was its construction. As explained above, aluminium alloys were unsuitable for the main parts of the airframe. In the USA, steel honeycomb and titanium were regarded as alternative substitutes in high-Mach aircraft; by 1960, quite large amounts of titanium had been used in a number of US aircraft (including the Vigilante), production facilities were in place, and it was possible to conceive of a small production run of all-titanium aircraft. The Soviet Union had less experience and fewer facilities. Moreover, the idea of mass-producing an all-titanium fighter by the mid-1960s was out of the question, as it would have been in the USA. Like Lockheed, the Mikoyan OKB had more sense than to try their luck with steel honeycomb.

What the Soviet Union did have was a great deal of experience with ordinary steel. Steel has never been part of the Western aircraft designer's culture, although steel alloys are cheap, have competitive strength-to-weight ratios – even at high temperatures – and are easy to work with. Aluminium is superior for most aircraft structures, because it is more ductile and more easily fabricated into large, light, load-bearing assemblies. It is also more tolerant of holes; thin aluminium sheet can be riveted, but steel of the same weight is too thin to stand such treatment, and demands welded joints which are mistrusted by the Western designer. Steel is more suited to concentrated loads, and, in 1960, had been used for, the frames and load-bearing bulkheads in all the Mikoyan jet fighters.

Structural materials

The Ye-26, therefore, was mainly built out of high-strength steel alloys. Most of the structure was arc-welded: the skins were stiffened with welded-on steel stringers, and welding was used to build up complex structural components that, in a Western type, would be forged. Forged steel was used for spars and main structural members; titanium was used for the leading edges and around the tailpipes, where the temperatures were highest; and some cooler parts, such as the trailing edges, flaps and ailerons, were of aluminium.

The structure weight, in total, came to 17 per cent more than that of the Vigilante, a similarly sized aircraft. This figure was respectable, but was achieved by carefully trading strength for weight. The Ye-26 was designed to pull a maximum of 5 g during the interception, when the fuel tanks would be much more than half empty; with full tanks, the maximum g was much lower. Most current fighters are designed to pull 9 g with full fuel, so their airframes must be more than twice as strong as that of the Mikoyan fighter. Neither was the airframe stressed for high speeds at low level.

The fuel system represented a unique answer to the problems of heating and sealing associated with high-speed operations: the designers simply abandoned integral tanks in favour of discrete fuel tanks built from continuously welded steel sheet. The system added some weight, but it was virtually leakproof, was easily fitted with a nitrogen inerting system, and furthermore insulated the fuel from the worst of the skin heating. In theory, the tanks reduced internal fuel volume; in practice, the 31,000lb (14,000kg) fuel load was 41 per cent of

clean gross weight, an excellent figure.

The propulsion system, as noted above, was based on a modified Tumansky missile engine. It was a single-shaft, fixed-geometry engine with five compressor stages and a single turbine stage without air cooling: its basic layout resembled a small jet engine such as a Rolls-Royce Viper. Static pressure ratio – the usual measure of an engine's efficiency – was only 7:1, considerably less than that of the MiG-21 powerplant. Despite its simplicity, the engine was large: its mass flow of 275-300lb/sec (125-135kg/sec) put it in the same class as the biggest contemporary pure jets. It was mostly made of steel, with some titanium.

The engine, however, was merely the core of the powerplant. It breathed through a long convergent duct fed by a cavernous two-dimensional inlet; a spill door for excess air was located on top of the inlet, and a small flap on the lower lip could be drooped to admit more air at low speeds. Two ramps on the top surface of the inlet were deflected downward under hydraulic power and electronic control at high speed, to constrict the throat and control the pattern of shock waves in the duct. Further back along the duct were a group of vanes to smooth out irregularities in the airflow, and a system for injecting methanol and water into the airstream. (Some 1,100lb (500kg) of the mixture was carried in tanks in the fins, and fed to the inlets through external conduits.) The methanol mixture cooled the air as it evaporated, and allowed thrust to be increased within the engine's temperature limitations.

Behind the engine was a monstrous augmentor, 50 per cent larger in diameter than the engine itself, fed with fuel from four injection manifolds and with three concentric flameholders. Ignition was by a pilot burner on the rear of the engine, which was lit at all times. The convergent-divergent nozzle was driven by 12 hydraulic jacks.

Powerplant performance

A propulsion system of this type was a sluggard at low speed. The low pressure ratio translated into poor specific fuel consumption. It also meant that the 'core' had a poor thrust/weight ratio, because it produced little power in relation to its size and airflow. The gargantuan inlet and augmentor, too, represented little more than dead weight and parasite drag at subsonic speeds, where the inlet could not compress the air enough to run the augmentor efficiently.

High speeds were a different story. Compression in the inlet duct increased with the square of the speed, probably attaining ratios in excess of 30:1. Because of the engine's low pressure ratio, it could swallow the high-pressure air from the inlet without encountering astronomical thermal loads, and without having to be throttled back like a more com-

plex, high-pressure engine. The air expanded through the turbine, but only enough to drive the compressor, so the air leaving the back of the engine was still highly compressed. Also, because of the vast mass of air swallowed by the inlet, and the relatively small amount of fuel burnt in the engine, the efflux was still rich in oxygen. Further oxygen was provided by engine cooling air, drawn from the inlet.

Augmentor thrust

The entire system was geared to providing near-ideal conditions of temperature, pressure and oxygenation at the augmentor. In fact, the main function of the core was to further compress and heat the air, making the augmentor more efficient; at high speed, its contribution to thrust was small. Virtually all the thrust at high speed was generated by expansion through the convergent-divergent nozzle, driven by the combustion of massive quantities of fuel in the augmentor.

This type of powerplant has been called a 'turboramjet', or a 'supercharged ramjet', and the term is accurate to a degree. While the components of the propulsion system are the same as those of any supersonic turbojet, most of the compression is done in the inlet and most of the thrust is generated at the final nozzle, just as happens in a pure ramjet. Perhaps 'turboramjet' is appropriate, since the other type of powerplant to carry the name – in which the jet is switched out of the cycle at high speed – has never been flown.

Just how much sheer thrust this sort of engine can produce at high speed is best illustrated by example. The F-15, judged a high-speed fighter, weighs just over half as much as the MiG design, when both are carrying missiles and half internal fuel, but the MiG has only 12 per cent more static thrust, and moreover its missiles are far larger and less efficiently carried. Yet the Soviet type is 60 per cent faster, mainly because it has a completely different type of powerplant. This is no discredit to the F-15, which was designed with entirely different missions in mind, but points out the unique thrust-producing characteristics of the turboramjet engine.

The engine and augmentor were installed for early flight tests in a test-bed aircraft derived from the MiG tailed-delta series. Designated Ye-166, it flew in 1961 and set a series of speed and altitude records in the following year. It tested the engine up to the design Mach 2.8 maximum speed.

Meanwhile, work on the Ye-26 continued. The aircraft systems were mostly conventional: thanks to the limited supersonic endurance, the aerodynamic heat from the skin would not soak through every part of the aircraft, as it did on the contemporary A-12. Apart from a new high-temperature synthetic hydraulic fluid, and a special cooling system

Above: Groundcrew give scale to the heavyweight MiG-25, its tall verticals and mighty afterburners. One man is standing on the stabilizer, a testimony to the type's rugged construction.

for engine accessories – a single-pass methanol/water system was used to cool the generators, the hydraulic pumps, and the avionics, the hot liquid being dumped into the inlets – the systems could have been taken off any contemporary Soviet aircraft, with two hydraulic circuits for the flight controls and pneumatics for the brakes.

Development of the fire-control system and the missiles proceeded in parallel. Unquestionably the most advanced feature of the fire-control system was the datalink, which was one of the first airborne systems anywhere to use a digital computer. The task of the computer was to translate high-speed digital pulses, which were easy to send by radio, into analogue signals that the aircraft systems would understand, and vice versa. The 'downlink' carried the radar imagery from the aircraft to the ground controller; the 'uplink' transmitted steering com-

MiG-25 'Foxbat-A' cutaway

1 Ventral airbrake
2 Starboard tailplane (aluminium alloy trailing edge)
3 Steel tailplane spar
4 Titanium leading edge

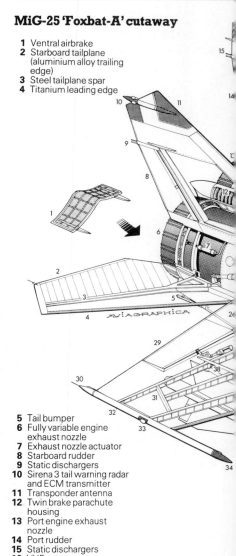

5 Tail bumper
6 Fully variable engine exhaust nozzle
7 Exhaust nozzle actuator
8 Starboard rudder
9 Static dischargers
10 Sirena 3 tail warning radar and ECM transmitter
11 Transponder antenna
12 Twin brake parachute housing
13 Port engine exhaust nozzle
14 Port rudder
15 Static dischargers
16 VHF antenna

mands from the ground control system to the autopilot. The pilot's task was to ensure that the aircraft and its systems were functioning properly, and he would not assume control until the aircraft's own radar had unambiguously locked on to the target.

Specialized radar

The radar itself was unusual. Unlike most airborne radars, it was not designed to detect or track the target: ground-based radar would have done so before the aircraft left the ground. Instead, its role was to provide a final, accurate fix on the target, in the face of extremely heavy jamming, to enable the pilot and ground controller to fly the aircraft into a position to launch missiles. The emphasis was on power: the radar was to be so powerful that even the reflection of the beam from the target would be stronger than any jamming signal. (The fighter radar was at an advantage, because its beam is concentrated, while jamming is seldom accurate in direction.)

'Burn-through' range varies with the radar cross-section of the target, and the power and efficiency of its jamming systems, but the Ye-26 radar was probably designed to acquire a B-70 at about 50nm (90km), in order to give accurate guidance over at least the last 60sec of an interception, despite the speed of the interceptor and the target. Beam or collision attack was the normal tactic.

Given the size of a B-70 and an estimate of its jamming power, combined with a radar power of 600kW, at least three times more than any previous fighter radar. Transistor technology was then in its early stages, so – rather like some hi-fi buffs of the same era – the Soviet designers elected to stay with vacuum tubes. These, however, had to meet new requirements: the sheer power of the new radar, combined with the heat in the nose of a Mach 3 aircraft; and the stresses incurred in going from arctic cold on a Siberian runway to maximum operat-

ing temperature in under ten minutes. The result was the biggest fighter radar ever built, weighing over 1,100lb (500kg). Another, theoretical drawback of the radar – a direct result of its high power – was that powerful ground clutter rendered it ineffective against targets below 1,650ft (500m) altitude.

Other systems aboard the MiG-25 were designed to resist or offset jamming. Communications were assured by large flush antennas in the fin, and emissions from hostile radars were detected by an electronic surveillance measures (ESM) system housed in slim wingtip pods. A final touch was a small optical sight in the cockpit: if all else failed and the B-70's mighty Westinghouse ECM system did its duty, the pilot had one last chance to get parameters with his IR missiles.

The missiles were of similarly heroic proportions, though range was not the reason for their size: the need for lethality and assured performance was more important, and each missile carried a 220lb (100kg) high-explosive/fragmentation warhead. The requirement to destroy a Mach 3 target pushed the weapon's speed upward, to Mach 4 or more, while the high operating altitude dictated large wings for the sake of manoeuvrability. All of these requirements drove the size and drag of the missile up. The resulting missile was twice as large as any Western AAM, and in fact was slightly bigger than a Hawk SAM.

Uniquely, the missile has three exhaust nozzles, two smaller nozzles being located on the body sides level with the wing trailing edges. Almost certainly, this indicates the use of a two-stage propulsion system, with a booster in the tail and a sustainer exhausting through side nozzles (see photo overleaf).

The missile was built in two versions: semi-active-radar (SAR) or infra-red (IR), and according to most accounts the normal operating technique is to fire one of each type in close succession. While

IR is normally considered to have a limited range, this particular weapon was designed for use against a large Mach 3 aircraft – its entire airframe radiating at 220-330°C – at high altitudes, where the normal attenuation of IR radiation with distance would be sharply reduced due to the thin air. The maximum range for effective missile launch was probably in the 25nm (50km) range, giving just enough time for a second salvo in a single pass should the first miss its mark.

While the entire system was still in the earliest stages of development, what could have been a fatal blow descended: the US Government cancelled the B-70 production programme. The first cancellation came in December 1959; a reprieve came in mid-1960, but the new Kennedy Administration wasted no time in putting a final halt to SAC's plans for deploying a Mach 3 bomber. Nevertheless, development of a system to shoot it down continued, although at a slightly more relaxed pace.

There were several reasons for this decision. The B-70 was still in being as a prototype programme, so the cancellation could still conceivably be reversed. The performance of the new fighter would also be useful against the B-58 and any successor aircraft; in 1960, the possibility of further B-58 production and development still existed. In all probability, too, the Soviet intelligence community knew that another long-range Mach 3 aircraft was under development in the USA, in the shape of the Lockheed A-12. A mock-up of a version of this aircraft with internal bays for nuclear weapons or reconnaissance sensors was completed in mid-1962, and following the Cuban missile crisis in October of that year it was ordered into production. The RS-71 would have full global range, with refuelling, and an equivalent bombload to the B-58. From the Soviet viewpoint, therefore, the threat of a high-altitude, high-Mach strategic attack force did not vanish with the cancellation of the B-70.

The first Ye-26 was flown in 1964. One early prototype, the Ye-266 set a 1,000km (540nm) closed-circuit speed record in April 1965, sustaining 1,252kt (2,320km/h) with a 4,410lb (2,000kg) payload. In those days, high-resolution satellite imagery of Soviet test centres was not available, so no inkling of the new type's shape appeared until July 9, 1967, when two of the aircraft appeared at the Aviation Day display at Domodedovo, near Moscow. They were officially described as being in the Mach 3 class, and confirmation of that performance came in October, when the Soviet Union claimed 500km (270nm) and 1,000km (540nm) closed-circuit records at speeds around Mach 2.8.

Record performance

The records beat the closed-circuit speeds set by the YF-12A (a member of the A-12 family) in May 1965, but there were two significant points which most observers missed. The YF-12A's 500km speed was slower than its 1,000km record, indicating that turning capability, rather than high-speed endurance, was the limiting factor. In the case of the Ye-26, the reverse was true: the 500km record was faster, showing that the aircraft was near its speed and endurance limits. The other observation that nobody made was that the Soviet team had not beaten the YF-12's 80,257ft (24,462m) altitude mark, or its Mach 3.12 straight-line speed record.

Instead, Western analysts tended to assume that, like the YF-12, the Ye-26 was much faster in the straight line than in the circuit, and was probably capable of Mach 3.2 or more. They also mirror-imaged the construction of the YF-12, and assumed that the Ye-26 had an ad-

Below: An uncomplicated cutaway reflects basic simplicity of design, with forged steel structural members and titanium used mainly for high-temperature secondary structure.

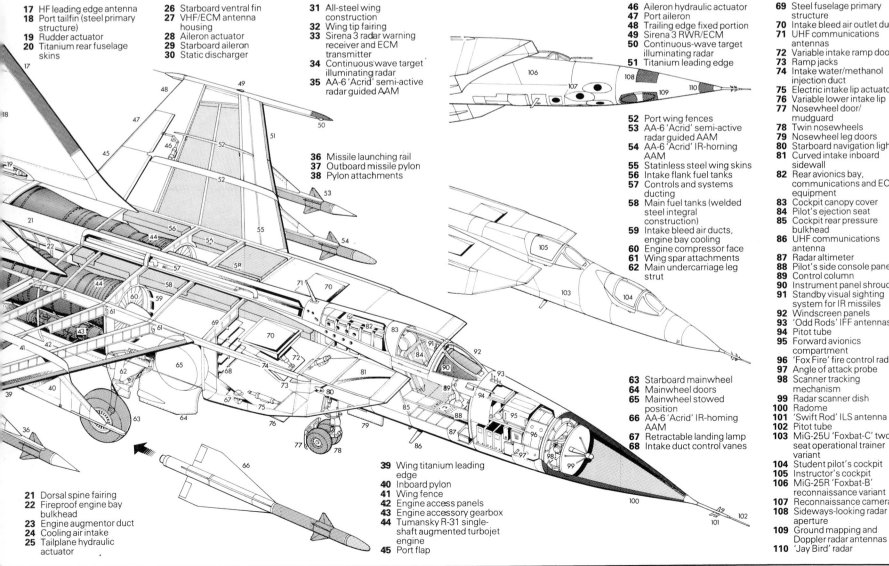

17 HF leading edge antenna
18 Port tailfin (steel primary structure)
19 Rudder actuator
20 Titanium rear fuselage skins
21 Dorsal spine fairing
22 Fireproof engine bay bulkhead
23 Engine augmentor duct
24 Cooling air intake
25 Tailplane hydraulic actuator

26 Starboard ventral fin
27 VHF/ECM antenna housing
28 Aileron actuator
29 Starboard aileron
30 Static discharger

31 All-steel wing construction
32 Wing tip fairing
33 Sirena 3 radar warning receiver and ECM transmitter
34 Continuous wave target illuminating radar
35 AA-6 'Acrid' semi-active radar guided AAM
36 Missile launching rail
37 Outboard missile pylon
38 Pylon attachments
39 Wing titanium leading edge
40 Inboard pylon
41 Wing fence
42 Engine access panels
43 Engine accessory gearbox
44 Tumansky R-31 single-shaft augmented turbojet engine
45 Port flap

46 Aileron hydraulic actuator
47 Port aileron
48 Trailing edge fixed portion
49 Sirena 3 RWR/ECM
50 Continuous-wave target illuminating radar
51 Titanium leading edge
52 Port wing fences
53 AA-6 'Acrid' semi-active radar guided AAM
54 AA-6 'Acrid' IR-homing AAM
55 Stainless steel wing skins
56 Intake flank fuel tanks
57 Controls and systems ducting
58 Main fuel tanks (welded steel integral construction)
59 Intake bleed air ducts, engine bay cooling
60 Engine compressor face
61 Wing spar attachments
62 Main undercarriage leg strut
63 Starboard mainwheel
64 Mainwheel doors
65 Mainwheel stowed position
66 AA-6 'Acrid' IR-homing AAM
67 Retractable landing lamp
68 Intake duct control vanes

69 Steel fuselage primary structure
70 Intake bleed air outlet duct
71 UHF communications antennas
72 Variable intake ramp doors
73 Ramp jacks
74 Intake water/methanol injection duct
75 Electric intake lip actuator
76 Variable lower intake lip
77 Nosewheel door/mudguard
78 Twin nosewheels
79 Nosewheel leg doors
80 Starboard navigation light
81 Curved intake inboard sidewall
82 Rear avionics bay, communications and ECM equipment
83 Cockpit canopy cover
84 Pilot's ejection seat
85 Cockpit rear pressure bulkhead
86 UHF communications antenna
87 Radar altimeter
88 Pilot's side console panel
89 Control column
90 Instrument panel shroud
91 Standby visual sighting system for IR missiles
92 Windscreen panels
93 'Odd Rods' IFF antennas
94 Pitot tube
95 Forward avionics compartment
96 'Fox Fire' fire control radar
97 Angle of attack probe
98 Scanner tracking mechanism
99 Radar scanner dish
100 Radome
101 'Swift Rod' ILS antenna
102 Pitot tube
103 MiG-25U 'Foxbat-C' two-seat operational trainer variant
104 Student pilot's cockpit
105 Instructor's cockpit
106 MiG-25R 'Foxbat-B' reconnaissance variant
107 Reconnaissance cameras
108 Sideways-looking radar aperture
109 Ground mapping and Doppler radar antennas
110 'Jay Bird' radar

vanced, lightweight, all-titanium airframe. The result was that Western estimates of empty weight were almost 25 per cent too low, and estimates of normal gross weight were almost 35 per cent low.

Another snare for Western analysts lay in the engine installation. The mass flow of the R-266 was, coincidentally, about the same as that of an advanced augmented turbofan engine of the same thrust rating. It was all too easy to believe that a high-pressure-ratio turbofan provided the Ye-26's motive power.

The impact of this assumption on estimates of range and transonic thrust/weight ratio was profound: as noted above, the R-266 is very inefficient outside the maximum speed regime, but a turbojet or turbofan would have been far better. Western estimates generally credited the Ye-26 with a normal combat radius of 600nm (1,120km), equal to that of an F-4 with maximum external fuel. The analysts then combined their thrust/weight ratio with their wing loading (which, along with the weight, was much too low) and deduced that the Ye-266 would be well able to hold its own in close-in combat. It was also naturally assumed that only an advanced pulse-Doppler radar would account for the large size of the Ye-26 radome.

Threat inflation

The final element in the 'Foxbat' myth was that from 1968 to 1972 the West thought that the Ye-26 was the MiG-23. Reports of preparations for large-scale MiG-23 production may well have reached the West, and further confused the picture. The Soviet Union made no attempt to dispel the confusion.

The result was that the Ye-26 – now codenamed 'Foxbat' by NATO – became the classic case of threat inflation. Combined with the accurately estimated dimensions, the known record-breaking flights and the quoted engine thrust, the picture that emerged was of a combat aircraft which sacrificed little efficiency or versatility in return for unmatched speed and altitude performance.

The USAF – then in the process of writing its requirements for a new tactical fighter – proved particularly susceptible to 'Foxbat' hysteria. The original F-X specification, which would have produced something like an F-18, was hastily revised to demand a top speed of Mach 2.5 and more radar detection range. The higher speed meant that complex variable-geometry inlets were needed, while the demand for improved radar implied a larger antenna, a wider forward fuselage and, ultimately, a heavier aircraft. The resulting aircraft, the F-15, is generally considered the Porsche 928 of fighters: supreme in performance and handling, full of sophisticated equipment, and so expensive that hardly anybody can afford it. It could be argued that the Ye-26 made its most significant contribution to the East-West military balance before flight tests were completed.

Meanwhile, development of the real Ye-26 proceeded rather more slowly than previous Soviet fighter programmes, partly because of its high performance and partly because of its complexity. There seems to have been no problem in attaining the required flight performance, as the 1967 records showed, but stability and control were clearly a problem area. Large-area ventral fins, operating in the high-pressure zone beneath the fuselage, were apparent on the aircraft shown at Domodedovo, and proved partially effective. One prototype tested endplate fins on the wingtips, which further improved directional stability at high speeds. The final solution was more conventional: the vertical fins were substantially enlarged, being increased in area by some 50 per cent, so that the leading edge overlapped the trailing edge of the wing, and the ventral fins were retained but considerably reduced in size.

Other detail differences apparent on at least one of the Ye-26 prototypes included a low-drag conformal fuel tank of about 175gal (800lit) recessed into the belly of the aircraft, and two small struts connecting the fuselage nose to the lower lips of the inlets, perhaps intended to solve a vibration problem.

Production of the new type apparently started in 1968, but was suspended after a senior PVO officer was killed in the crash of a Ye-26 prototype; it was resumed about a year later, and the type entered service in 1970-71 with the service designation MiG-25. It is possible that the armament initially comprised AA-5 'Ash' missiles, as used on the Tu-28P 'Fiddler' interceptor, but the missile specially developed for the aircraft,

Above: Apparent in this view of a Libyan MiG-25 are the three propulsion nozzles of the AA-6 missile, which have passed unnoticed in all previous publications. The two small nozzles on the sides of the missile, between the wings, are probably the exhausts of the cruise motor, the booster being in the tail.

known to NATO as AA-6 'Acrid', was in service by 1975. The basic interceptor version was known to NATO as 'Foxbat-A'; its radar was identified as 'Fox Fire'.

As is normal Soviet practice, a conversion/proficiency trainer version entered service in parallel, the MiG-25U adding a second cockpit in the nose, ahead of the normal cockpit – the fuselage aft was too narrow – and this replaced the fire-control system and radar.

The MiG-25, with its supporting ground environment, was certainly the best high-altitude interception system of its day. In service, it turned out to meet the requirements laid down for it, and it would probably have been effective against the B-70. Lockheed's Skunk Works, however, had gone one better than the Soviet planners had anticipated: cruising at altitudes up to 95,000ft (29,000m), the SR-71 was safely outside the MiG-25/AA-6 envelope. But the USAF had no way of knowing this, and the presumed capability of the MiG-25 was a major factor in the US Government's decision not to use SR-71s or D-21 drones for penetrations of Soviet airspace, denying itself – in the words of USAF intelligence chief Gen George Keegan – 'vast amounts of intelligence.'

Given the success of the basic design, the lack of high-altitude targets and the Soviet Union's lack of a high-flying reconnaissance aircraft, it was logical to adapt the MiG-25 for such a mission. The MiG-25R entered service in parallel with the basic interceptor; it was identical up to the front cockpit wall, and in aerodynamic shape, but the nosecone contained a much smaller forward-looking radar, probably related to the MiG-21's 'Jay Bird'. This made space and payload available for a useful sensor package.

Two versions of the type have been observed: 'Foxbat-B', with conventional and video cameras and side-looking radar, and the electronic intelligence (elint) 'Foxbat-D', without cameras, but with a more extensive array of flush-mounted antennas. Both versions use the advanced datalink to relay real-time information to ground stations, and may be guided from ground stations.

A small group of MiG-25Rs were deployed to Cairo West, Egypt, in 1971 as part of the Soviet expeditionary force, remaining there until 1974. Without missiles, and possibly using drop tanks, the MiG-25R had better range and altitude performance than the fully loaded fighter. Between October 1971 and March 1972, MiG-25Rs based at Cairo covered the Israeli-held coastline from Haifa to Port Said, and flew the length of the Sinai Peninsula, both missions calling for 270nm (500km) penetrations of Israeli airspace and a total range in the region of 500nm (900km). Longer missions were flown at slightly reduced speeds, around Mach 2.5, but combined with the 80,000ft (24,000m) cruising altitude they were enough to confound Israel's air defences.

Flights and interception attempts continued into 1973. One MiG-25R was tracked at Mach 3.2 over Sinai, and the word soon went around the souks that the aircraft barely made it back to base, its engines having suffered severe damage. It was not appreciated at the time that this was the normal and inevitable consequence of flight outside normal speed limits.

In the same year, in June and July, the Ye-266 captured a series of time-to-height records, reaching 98,430ft (30,000m) in 4min 4sec and attaining a peak altitude of 118,900ft (36,240m), far higher than any aircraft had ever gone without rocket boost. The McDonnell Douglas F-15 Streak Eagle took the time-to-height records in January-February 1975, but in May the Ye-266 struck back and regained the title. The aircraft used for the 1975 records was designated Ye-266M, and apparently used RD-F engines rated at 31,000lb (14,000kg) thrust. (Not too much reliance should be placed on such numbers, because the thrust of the original engines was never accurately stated in record claims.) McDonnell Douglas analyzed the Soviet figures, and has claimed that they could not have been achieved without rocket boost.

The time-to-height records gave the 'Foxbat' myth another boost, but worse was to come. In mid-1975, 'Foxbat-Bs' were deployed to Poland, making some sorties to East Germany. Immediately afterward, NATO surveillance radars started tracking Mach 2.8 targets emanating from Poland at 90,000ft (27,430m) altitude, flying as far as the North Atlantic ports and returning at the same speed. In the light of such observations, even the original estimates of the MiG-25's range seemed low; the tracking data suggested an operational radius of 650nm (1,200km) at sustained high-supersonic speed. From this, one analyst deduced that the MiG-25 should be capable of a 1,080nm (2,000km) radius fighter mission, cruising at Mach 2.2 and including 2min combat. This was awesome performance indeed, suggesting that Polish-based MiG-25s could present a threat to NATO aircraft as far away as the Greenland-Iceland-UK gap.

The scare had been caused by a simple confusion. Western intelligence was entirely unaware that the Soviet Union's reconnaissance formations had deployed a new surveillance drone with a Mach 2.8 cruise speed and a range of about 1,600nm (3,000km). Derived from Soviet cruise-missile technology, it was launched from a mobile ramp and recovered by parachute. The MiG-25s based in Poland, as well as being tasked with high-altitude probes into Western airspace, formed the perfect cover for this new system.

'Foxbats' for export

Then came Hakodate, and the legend was punctured. With the MiG-25's cover blown, it became available to trusted export customers such as Algeria, Libya and Syria, which took delivery of the 'Foxbat-A' complete with AA-6 missiles in 1979-80. In 1982, India replaced its ageing Canberra PR.9s with eight MiG-25Rs. The reconnaissance aircraft are certainly useful, but it is hard to see what purpose the fighter variants serve apart from prestige. The 'Flogger-B/G', with its greater endurance, is unquestionably a better all-round fighter against the targets such nations are likely to face. And even the MiG-25 is not invulnerable, as the Israeli Defence Force-Air Force demonstrated in June 1982. Two Syrian MiG-25s were destroyed over Lebanon, probably by well-planned 'snap-up' F-15/Sparrow attacks.

Most of the Soviet MiG-25 fighter fleet – some 300 aircraft strong – has been retrofitted to 'Foxbat-E' configuration, with the same radar/missile system as the MiG-23. The 'High Lark' radar and IR search-and-track set give improved capability against manoeuvring and low-altitude targets, of the type which the MiG-25 is now more likely to face. The 'Foxbat-E' also features an extended tail bullet, probably indicating the presence of upgraded electronic countermeasures equipment. 'Foxbat-E' fighters based in Eastern Europe have been scrambled in response to SR-71 flights along the East-West border, and pose a significant threat to NATO air assets such as E-3 Awacs aircraft.

The 'Foxbat-E' represents an interim step to the ultimate development of the line, which responds to the B-1 as the original responded to the B-70: the MiG-31 'Foxhound', discussed later in the book. Its significance now, 25 years after the design of the original MiG-25 got under way, is material testimony to the outstanding qualities of the original design.

MiG-29 'Fulcrum'

Still largely a mystery to the West, partly because of a lengthy and perhaps difficult development process, but mainly because of the effectiveness of Soviet security precautions, the MiG-29 'Fulcrum' represents the state of the art in Soviet fighter design. There is little doubt that few, if any, key aviation technologies developed in the West have gone unmatched in the Soviet Union, and the MiG-29 will, like the MiG-21, MiG-23 and MiG-25 before it, represent a massive advance over earlier Soviet fighters. What remains to be seen is whether such a complex aircraft can match their outstanding producibility.

Above: Satellite reconnaissance is able to produce early and good planform data, but other details can remain uncertain. This sketch of a MiG-29, released in April 1984 by the US Department of Defense, suggests an F-18-like fuselage geometry with lateral inlets built into the fuselage sides.

Of all the new combat aircraft to appear in the 1960s, the MiG-23 was by far the most successful. While the Mikoyan swing-wing fighter was built in thousands, new Western types in that decade were overshadowed by the continued dominance of the F-4 and Mirage, designs which dated back to the 1950s. In the 1970s, as a consequence, Western and Soviet fighter developments were out of phase. Mass production of the MiG-23/27 series dominated the Soviet scene: in the West, a generation of new fighters appeared to replace the F-4, Mirage and F-104 as the primary tactical combat aircraft.

The new Western types were characterized by an emphasis on long-neglected qualities, particularly manoeuvrability in the high-subsonic regime and pilot visibility. This was not a fad: it reflected a careful analysis of combat experience in Vietnam, the Middle East and other theatres. Two fundamental lessons had emerged from this analysis.

One lesson was that beyond-visual-range (BVR) combat was much more difficult than the analysts of the 1950s had believed. Speed, confusion, fog of battle, unreliable IFF, low altitudes, better ECM, radar warning systems and the sheer complexity of the BVR radar/missile guidance loop all tended to diminish the probability that the first long-range salvo of BVR missiles would hit their targets. IR-homing missiles were more reliable, and guns were better still, but both had to be used in close combat.

Energy for combat

The second lesson was that success in air combat was highly dependent on energy. The typical fighter of the 1950s entered the ring fast and high, with a great deal of momentum, but as it turned to close on an enemy's tail its weight and its small wing told against it, and its momentum began to bleed away faster than its engines could put it back. The fighter quickly began to lose speed, height and the initiative.

The Western fighters of the 1970s had efficient, relatively long-span wings for good turning performance, and – equally important – light and extremely powerful new engines. While their predecessors could generate an instantaneous 7g break *in extremis*, these new machines could turn at 9g until they ran out of fuel.

It is not in the nature of the Soviet system to emulate the West as a matter of habit. But facts are facts, and as the details of the new F-15 and F-14 emerged in the early 1970s it must have become increasingly clear that, even in small numbers, they posed a problem for the MiG-23. The Soviet type would be at a disadvantage in the BVR phase, but even if

this proved indecisive – the best one could hope for – the US fighters would almost literally fly rings around their adversary in close combat. Despite major modifications applied in advance of production, the MiG-23 was an inherently poor dogfighter, becoming steadily more stable (harder to manoeuvre) at increasing speeds.

Against the smaller F-16, the MiG-23 has an undisputed first-shot advantage. But this is significant only in the uncertain world of BVR, and in close combat the MiG-23 is, once again, outclassed. If the F-16 pilot can evade or spoof the first BVR salvo, he immediately more than reverses the MiG-23's advantage.

Another steadily increasing threat (as viewed from the Soviet side) has been the ability of NATO to operate at very low level. When the MiG-23 was conceived, it was generally considered that ultra-low-altitude operations, 250ft (75m) or less above the treetops, would be the province of a few specialized and expensive aircraft. The Royal Air Force, however, showed that single-seat attack fighters could operate 'down in the weeds', given an inertial navigation system and a head-up display. This tactic put most of NATO's attack aircraft out of the MiG-23's BVR envelope; during the 1980s, new systems will extend ultra-low-level flight to night operations.

All these developments in the threat emerged in the late 1960s. In a way, the timing was awkward for the Soviet Union. Although the trend in technology and operations was clearly apparent, there was no practical alternative to the MiG-23: any new fighter reflecting combat lessons would take years to develop, and would not be available in quantity until the late 1970s, while to rely on the MiG-21 and Su-7 for so long was unthinkable. The MiG-23 was made the subject of a major production programme, alongside new versions of the MiG-21 and Su-7.

The next generation

New fighters in the post-Vietnam mould were accordingly deferred to the next generation. Serious planning probably started in 1971-72, giving rise to an operational requirement in 1973-74. While there is no way of knowing exactly what planning steps were taken, subsequent events make it possible to reconstruct the planners' logic.

Agile fighters and low-level attack aircraft were, in all probability, two of the most important factors taken into account. A look-down, shoot-down (LDSD) radar/missile system, capable of engaging fighter-size targets in ground clutter, was a basic requirement. This meant a sophisticated radar, with a lar-

Above: The latest DoD impression of the MiG-29 suggests a cross between an F-16 and an F-14, with ventral inlets and separate engine nacelles. Details, either sensitive or unknown, are coyly hidden behind a quartet of R-23R missiles. It also shows tailbooms carrying the fins and tailerons.

ger antenna than that of the F-16; in fact, there was probably little chance of making the system smaller than the MiG-23 radar. The missiles would also be larger than simple IR-homing weapons. All of this tended to drive the weight of the aircraft upwards. Comparable agility to the F-16 and F-15 was also required.

Up to this point, the requirement was not too demanding for an aircraft which would appear some years after the US fighters. However, the new aircraft was also planned to match the range and speed of the MiG-23. The high installed thrust dictated by manoeuvrability objectives made it more difficult to achieve a long range, while a Mach 2.3 speed requirement added weight – in the form of variable inlets, for example – and complicated the aerodynamic design. The requirement could be met, but only by an aircraft as big as an F-15, something which would put the basic Soviet requirement for numerical superiority far out of reach.

US Department of Defense analysts currently believe that the Soviet Union solved the dilemma by developing two aircraft: a large, F-15-sized aircraft for the long-range fighter mission, and a smaller, less costly type, differing mainly in having a shorter range, and intended for both air-to-air and strike missions. The larger aircraft is the Sukhoi Su-27 'Flanker', while the latter is the newest Mikoyan type, the MiG-29 'Fulcrum'.

It should be noted that this explanation of the two types' design missions is not universally accepted. It has been suggested that the Su-27 may be intended for use on the Soviet Union's new aircraft carrier, as well as on land; and there may be other workable hypotheses. The DoD view certainly smacks of 'mirror imaging', reflecting the way that the USAF uses the F-15 and F-16, while the MiG-29 and the F-16 are two very different aircraft.

RAM-L in production

A prototype or technology demonstrator for the MiG-29 started flight tests at Ramenskoye, near Moscow, in 1977, and was initially known in the West as RAM-L. (If early Western figures were reasonably accurate, this aircraft may have been smaller than the production aircraft, with a maximum take-off weight in the F-16A class, and with R-13 or R-25 engines.) By early 1979 the RAM-L was considered to be a strong candidate for production, and by mid-1982 it was known that production was under way. An operational test unit formed in late 1983, and full production started in 1984 at a plant near Moscow.

Early Western impressions of RAM-L showed a basic configuration similar to that of the Northrop P530/YF-17/F-18, with very large leading-edge root extensions (Lerxes) reaching to the nose. In 1981-82, however, nearly all sources, including USAF and DoD publications, showed a modified MiG-25 shape, with smaller Lerxes and vertical-ramp inlets, and it was not until the trials unit formed that the public consensus settled on the original Northrop-type configuration.

The starting point for the MiG-29 design was clearly the MiG-25, from which it derived its wing sweep and aspect ratio and the relative size and location of its tail surfaces. This may seem odd, because the MiG-25 is no dogfighter: but it was designed to manoeuvre in the very difficult high-Mach, high-altitude environment, where some of the problems, such as high angles of attack and low

control power, are surprisingly similar to those encountered in medium-altitude air combat. It is also a compact, low-drag configuration in which most of the main aerodynamic loads are conveniently concentrated in the close-coupled rear and centre fuselage.

Plan-view drawings of the MiG-29 suggest that the only trailing-edge control surfaces are set well inboard. This implies that the horizontal tail provides the primary roll control, perhaps with the aid of spoilers at low speed, and that the wing surfaces are plain flaps. There is no sign of the full-span leading-edge and trailing-edge flaps, operable over the entire flight envelope, that are found on the F-16 and F-18.

The main aerodynamic difference between the MiG-25 and the MiG-29 is the addition of Lerxes. These sharply swept surfaces do several things to help the aircraft manoeuvre. Their main characteristics are their high sweep and low aspect ratio: taken together, these mean that they have little effect in level flight, and develop progressively more lift as the aircraft pitches upward. Like a delta wing, the Lerx provides a smooth increase in lift with increasing pitch, and does not stall in the conventional way. At high angles of attack, it also sheds a strong vortex over the upper surface of the wing.

As the aircraft turns, the Lerx provides a gradual increase in lift, destabilizing the aircraft and reducing the amount of stabilizer downforce needed to sustain the turn. The effective wing loading and the induced drag are also reduced, and the spanwise lift distribution becomes more biased towards the centreline, reducing bending moments on the wing. At the same time, the vortex shed by the Lerx inhibits spanwise flow, and helps to prevent tip stall. The vortex generates its own low-pressure region over the wing, and provides a powerful lift boost of its own.

There are as many different patterns of Lerx as there are design teams working the problem. The MiG-29 Lerx (also used on the Su-27) is one of the simplest, forming a highly swept, straight-edged extension of the wing. Lerx design is not easy, introducing problems such as interaction of the vortices and the vertical tails, and involving what one distinguished Western designer has called the 'black art' of vortex lift. Lerxes similar to those on the MiG-29 appear on Northrop P530 studies dated 1968; the much more complex curved shape used on later de-

signs and, eventually, on the F-18, was substituted in the following year, because it was considered to provide more lift and a better vortex.

The size of the Lerxes suggests strongly that the MiG-29, like the F-16 and F-18, is unstable in pitch – that is to say, the aerodynamic centre may be ahead of the centre of gravity some or all of the time. This brings considerable advantages: in level flight, the tail is providing an upward force, contributing to lift rather than subtracting from it, so that the drag usually caused by tail downforce is absent. In a sustained turn, where the normal lift and downforce are multiplied by the g load, relaxed stability provides even greater benefits.

If the MiG-29 is pitch-unstable, as seems likely, it must have full-time, redundant artificial stability, probably provided by an electronically signalled – 'fly-by-wire' (FBW) – flight control system. This could have been the first system of its type on a Soviet aircraft, but

Above: The relationship of the MiG-29 planform to that of the MiG-25 is apparent in the plan view: the size, shape and relative positions of the wings, tailerons and ventral fins are all similar.

the technology was mature enough to be used on the An-124 transport, flown at the end of 1982.

The uncertainties involved in Lerx design and the technical risks of FBW may account for the West's confusion over the MiG-29's basic layout in 1981-82. It is the author's view that at least one prototype was completed in a lower-risk, naturally stable back-up configuration with smaller Lerxes, MiG-25-type inlets and a conventional mechanically signalled control system. Another reason for testing such a type could lie in inlet design. The MiG-25 inlet is one of the most efficient designs for high Mach numbers and high angles of attack, but is difficult to combine with a full-length Lerx because of its length and width. A fly-off between two similar aircraft would have clearly brought out the strengths and weaknesses of the two.

The size of the MiG-29 is set by the need to carry an LDSD radar/missile system, with the result that it is much bigger than the F-16, and slightly larger and more powerful than the F/A-18. It is also large enough to have two engines as a matter of necessity rather than choice. The fuselage layout is reminiscent of the F-15, in that the engines are set widely apart, on either side of the main keel. One difference in favour of the Soviet

Mikoyan MiG-29 'Fulcrum'

This provisional drawing of the MiG-29 was prepared in the first half of 1985, based on information from a variety of sources. It should be noted that many of these contradict each other, and that no clear and unambiguous description of the aircraft had been released to any unclassified source at the time of writing. Similarly, details of the AA-X-10 missile, said to make up the primary armament of the new fighter, are not yet available.

design, though, is that the swept, canted fins and the canted stabilizer trunnions make it possible to attach all the tail surfaces directly to the rear fuselage, eliminating the tailbooms seen on the F-15. The spacing of the engines allows straight ducts from the underwing inlets – possibly of the MiG-23-style vertical-ramp type – to the engines, and provides a wide track for a simple landing gear. The width of the forward fuselage is set by the radar, and it may taper in plan view towards the rear, like that of the MiG-25. The canopy design does not seem to offer quite as much unobstructed visibility as that of the new US fighters.

Structural details are uncertain. The Soviet Union has worked extensively on composite materials, particularly carbon (graphite) fibres. However, titanium is abundant in the Soviet Union, and the country has a great deal of processing capacity, so it may make a more attractive alternative to carbon-fibre materials than it does in the West. One Soviet brochure, interestingly, shows a carbon-fibre-skinned honeycomb taileron similar to that of the MiG-29. Given the nature of the Soviet system – in particular, the fact that technology usually responds to a clear and definite need – it might be

Above: It is likely that the MiG-29 will carry a large and powerful radar/missile suite, and an IRST set. At the same time, all-round vision may not attain the same levels as on the fighter's US contemporaries.

surprising to find a great deal of composite structure on the MiG-29. The required performance can be achieved with aluminium, steel and titanium.

The MiG-29 is, not surprisingly, powered by a pair of Tumansky engines. These are of a new type, designated R-33D, and are reported to be the first augmented turbofans to be used on a Soviet fighter. A very low bypass ratio, minimizing cost and handling problems, is to be expected.

Details of the avionics carried by the MiG-29 are sketchy. The radome diameter, one external indication of the potential of the forward-looking radar, is in the same class as the F-15 and MiG-23. US sources have ascribed a 60nm (110km) search range and a 45nm (83km) tracking range to the MiG-29 radar, but this figure is hard to evaluate in the absence of a radar cross-section for the target. The MiG-29 is also likely to carry an improved version of the infrared tracker fitted to the MiG-23, and a

high-capacity, ECM-resistant datalink.

According to US sources, the MiG-29 is to be armed with the AA-10, a new missile with a 25nm (46km) range and an active terminal seeker. The total armament is quoted as six missiles but, as in the case of the MiG-31, the maximum load probably reflects a mix of BVR weapons and small dogfight missiles in the R-60 (AA-8 'Aphid') class.

The MiG-29 certainly carries at least one internal gun. Some plan views show two heavy-calibre single-barrel weapons above the Lerxes, in positions similar to that of the F-16's single M61A1. These would be more effective than the GSh-23 and lighter than the MiG-27's Gatling. The installation leaves the underside of the aircraft clean for external stores, and keeps the burnt gases well clear of the inlets.

Full-scale production of the MiG-29 is reported to have been delayed for about a year by technical problems, before starting in 1984. Remarkably, the Indian Air Force is scheduled to receive the type in 1985; the delivery of 45 complete aircraft will be followed by a licence-production programme at HAL's Nasik facility, where some 150 MiG-29s will be assembled or built, starting in 1987-88. The agreement to supply MiG-29s followed an urgent request from India for an aircraft capable of meeting Pakistan's F-16s on equal terms. The IAF aircraft, however, will carry two R-23 (AA-7 'Apex') and four R-60 missiles, and it would not be surprising to find an updated version of the 'High Lark' radar.

The DoD suspects that the MiG-29 may be used in the strike mission in the future. This is certainly possible: like current US fighters, the MiG-29 has a strong structure, a generously sized wing and plenty of power, and this means that it has the potential for carrying a large external load. The common-sense application of such ideas as conformal fuel tanks and tandem stores carriage. as used on the F-15E, would turn the MiG-29 into a capable attack aircraft. One question, however, is whether the full-up MiG-29, with its advanced radar and missiles, would be used for such a mission, or whether a strike version, analogous to the MiG-27, would be developed.

From what little we have seen of the MiG-29, it appears to be another crisp and economical response to a sensible requirement. Apparently comparable to the F-18, but slightly faster, it will certainly not be at a disadvantage in close-in combat against any modern aircraft. In a

dogfight, the numbers for the F-18, F-16 and MiG-29 are so similar that differences in tactics, pilot skill level and – very important – missile capability will prove decisive.

As it stands in 1985, the MiG-29's long-range armament and systems outclass those of the F-16, and are in the same category as those of the F-18. To some extent, too, its high altitude and speed may give it the ability to accept or refuse combat according to whether the tactical situation is favourable. Developments in Soviet fighter training and doctrine – de-emphasizing the textbook, and placing more stress on instant response, initiative and flexibility – will allow the Soviet Air Force to take full advantage of the type.

Production slow-down

One remaining question, though, will be answered only in the course of time. So far, fighter production rates in the Soviet Union have not returned to the levels reached in the late 1970s, having dipped in the early 1980s as four largely or completely new types – the MiG-29, MiG-31, Su-25 'Frogfoot' and Su-27 – entered production. The MiG-29 is undoubtedly a capable aircraft. It is also, by Soviet standards, a fairly complicated one, with its advanced radar and missile system and its twin engines. The same applies to the Su-27, only more so, and even the Su-25 is a twin-engined aircraft. The result is that if fighter output is to be maintained, engine output will have to be virtually doubled.

Again, three of the new types have advanced radars. As noted in the chapter of the MiG-23/27, production of the fully equipped fighter with the 'High Lark' look-down radar has only been a fraction of the whole, probably running at under 200 aircraft a year. The output of even more sophisticated radars will have to reach four times that level if fully equipped MiG-29s, MiG-31s and Su-27s form the bulk of production at 1970s rates. The delays in Su-27 and MiG-29 production reported by US sources in 1985 are therefore far from surprising, and output will almost certainly climb more slowly than US sources have implied.

Meanwhile, the total of comparable new-generation fighters in service with NATO and other Western allies is well over the 2,000 mark: in the light of this figure, the importance of the MiG-29's success to the Soviet Union is difficult to overstate.

MiG-31 'Foxhound'

Faced with a requirement for a new long-range interceptor able to detect, track and destroy low-visibility B-1 bombers carrying out their attacks at low levels, the Soviet Union appears to have selected a development of the fast, heavily armed but short-legged MiG-25. Looking at the likely shape of the requirement, and at the potential of the original design, however, it seems that a much altered MiG-25, with more efficient engines, new missiles and an improved radar and fire-control system, and with large external tanks for increased range, could form the basis for the world's most powerful interceptor.

Soviet territorial air defence

Above: US DoD map showing the Soviet Union's territorial air defence system. The MiG-31 will provide the

Politicians and public were quick to react when the MiG-25 'Foxbat-A' interceptor, as delivered to Japan by Lt Viktor Belenko, turned out to be spectacularly different from the aircraft that Western intelligence had described. It was, to say the least, a bad time for the credibility of such Western assessments. Perhaps in order to save face, it was leaked that Belenko had described an improved version of the MiG-25, which was undergoing flight tests at the time of his departure from the Soviet Union, and which might possess some of the threatening attributes that the real MiG-25 lacked.

This new aircraft is not known as well as the MiG-23 was known at a similar stage in its career. At the time of writing, no photograph of the type has been published. However, the US Department of Defense has released a general-arrangement drawing of the type, presumably derived from satellite observation (and, probably, from ground observation as well) which forms the basis for the following preliminary assessment.

'Foxbat' derivation

The new aircraft is now identified as the MiG-31 (although it appears to have preceded the MiG-29 into service) and carries the NATO reporting name 'Foxhound'. The most important single observation to be made from available evidence, however, is that the MiG-31 is very closely related to the MiG-25. It has been reported that its designation before service entry was MiG-25M, and this would not be surprising given the high commonality between the original version and its new development.

There is very little uncertainty about the MiG-31's primary role: it has clearly been developed to counter the USAF/Rockwell B-1 bomber, just as the MiG-25 was developed to intercept the B-70. Development of the B-1 was launched in the summer of 1970 – after several years of debate over what sort of performance would be required of a future bomber, if one was needed at all – and the type was due to become operational in the early 1980s.

To put it baldly, the B-1 threatened the entire Soviet air defence system with obsolescence, despite the billions of roubles which had been poured into it during the 1960s, and despite the fact that it was better equipped and vastly larger than any other air defence organization in the world. Unfortunately, none of its fighters or missiles had any ability to acquire a low-flying target against the ground, let alone track it or guide a missile on to it, while the B-1, with its fighter-type configuration and highly efficient turbofan engines, could fly at very low

altitudes throughout the Soviet Union.

Moreover, the B-1's design was not only efficient, but took account of investigations into reducing the radar cross-section (RCS) of an aircraft. This would make it even more difficult to find. The Soviet air defence system was particularly vulnerable to low-level penetration, because of the reliance placed on ground-controlled interception (GCI): if both the target and the pursuing aircraft dropped below the controller's radar horizon, the game was up.

At the end of 1972, the Soviet-supplied and Soviet-maintained air defence system of North Vietnam was put to its biggest test, as the Linebacker II raids sent dozens of B-52s directly over Hanoi. The loss of 14 B-52s, with others damaged, was regarded at the time as a defeat for the USAF; but for the Soviet interceptor community, Linebacker II was an unmitigated disaster. Faced with huge waves of heavily laden bombers, flying at high altitude in broad daylight over a complete air defence system, the MiG-21PF interceptors missed the lot: all the damage to the B-52 force was caused by SAMs. To add insult to injury, B-52 tail-gunners shot down at least two MiG-21s as they manoeuvred to fire their missiles.

The advent of the B-1 and the catastrophe of Linebacker II made a complete reform of the manned fighter component of the Soviet air defence system inevitable. (Missiles retained their target-defence role, within the existing organization.) The basic philosophy of using thousands of limited-range fighters, operating in many small cells under strict GCI rules, as the primary means of air defence had to be abandoned. This was to have a profound effect on the shape of the next interceptor.

The basic requirement for a new interceptor was presumably issued as the B-1 programme started, in 1970-71. Capability against low-visibility, low-level targets called for greater operating autonomy, a considerable search range and a look-down/shoot-down radar/missile system, and a two-man crew to operate the system. The result would automatically be a large, heavy and expensive aircraft. Most Western analysts would have bet on a derivative of the Su-24 being adapted fill that role, but it did not work out that way, for sound and fundamental reasons.

There is only one way to offset the advantage of surprise enjoyed by a low-altitude attacker, and that is to place the acquisition radar on an aircraft. In fact, the definition of an advanced airborne early warning and control (AEW&C) aircraft probably preceded that of an interceptor. The first-generation Tu-126

Below: The MiG-31 is heavier than the MiG-25, but its overall dimensions are about the same. The plan view shows that the length of the main fuselage has been considerably increased – the tailpipes have been extended aft, and the inlets forward – while room has been made for a second cockpit by widening the fuselage.

Interceptor bases ●

Strategic SAM concentrations ■

look-down/shoot-down capability essential to deal with the threat posed by the USAF's new B-1B bomber.

Above: Fast, stealthy and manoeuvrable, the USAF/Rockwell B-1B presents a difficult target at low altitude to even the most sophisticated air defence system. The ability of a well designed and properly equipped manned bomber to avoid detection and interception was confirmed during tests with the B-1 prototypes.

Mikoyan MiG-31 'Foxhound'

The DoD illustrations upon which this drawing is based show an aircraft directly derived from the MiG-25. In detail, the aircraft may differ more substantially from its predecessor, reflecting its lower design speed and greater range. However, it does appear to be a true derivative of the earlier design.

Above: The MiG-31 has been depicted with very large drop tanks on its outer pylons, but its primary weapon – the AA-9 missile – has not yet been seen in any unclassified presentation. However, it is generally described as bearing a close resemblance in size and performance to a late-model AIM-7 Sparrow. The eight-missile armament suggests that belly weapon stations are also available.

'Moss' – probably intended to provide AEW cover for the Soviet Navy, as much as anything else – had no look-down capability, and a much more sophisticated system would be required for strategic air defence. It would need an advanced radar and powerful digital computers to cope with the many real and false targets within its detection range. It would need sophisticated displays to help its human operators manage the air battle, and multiple data links to guide the fighters to the interception point. The entire system would have to be effective against a fast and wily adversary with a highly advanced jamming system and, quite possibly, the means to shoot back.

The result is that AEW&C types are the most expensive of all military aircraft, and are inevitably limited in numbers. The new Soviet AEW&C platform, the Ilyushin 'Mainstay-A' derived from the Il-76 freighter, is no exception. It is expected that no more than four will be built each year, and that a maximum of 50 may eventually enter service.

Even the best AEW&C aircraft can handle only a limited number of fighters and targets at any moment. Now, the rate at which these scarce systems can handle targets is directly related to the interval between the first detection of an intruder and the point at which the airborne controller 'hands off' the target to the fighter crew. In the Soviet environment the nearest fighter may easily be hundreds of miles away, so the fighter's speed becomes critical – and the MiG-

25's shape is remarkably efficient at supersonic speeds.

Endurance is less important. Most Soviet targets are deep inside Soviet territory, so it is possible to mount an effective air defence from usable bases on the perimeter. The fighters can either scramble and dash to the target area, or remain on patrol without ever straying far from a refuelling base.

Even with a relaxed range requirement, the MiG-25 might look like a non-starter. But its normal 160nm (300km) operational radius is mainly a result of the very high speeds which it attains, and the extremely poor efficiency of its engines outside their normal high-speed envelope. The short span and high wing loading are the only inherent disadvantages of the airframe; on the other hand, its internal fuel capacity is remarkably high. A reduction in dash speed makes it possible to use more conventional powerplants, which would be more advanced and efficient than the 1950s engines of the MiG-25, and for a mixed subsonic/supersonic mission the type could easily be modified to carry very large external fuel tanks. Such changes would increase combat radius to a remarkable degree.

The new aircraft, flown in 1974-75, appears to retain most of the MiG-25's structure. The wing, the tail surfaces and the entire centre-section seem basically unchanged, although the wing-tip avionics pods are gone, and small leading-edge root extensions (Lerxes) are added to the wings and vertical tails. The forward fuselage has been redesigned; both the fuselage and the inlet ducts have been extended by about 40in (100cm), and the fuselage between the inlets is wider, accommodating a second cockpit. The nose ahead of the cockpit is shorter than that of the MiG-25, and at the rear, the tailpipes extend about 60in (150cm) further aft.

According to the DoD, the MiG-31 has a maximum speed of Mach 2.4 This is an important figure. The MiG-25 powerplant was defined by the need for high thrust at high speed; a Mach 2.4 aircraft, however, could easily be powered by a conventional afterburning turbojet, corresponding to a scaled-up Tumansky R-29. Such an engine, with about 25 per cent more mass flow and thrust than the R-29, would be far more efficient in the cruise regime. It would also, in all probability, be slightly longer than the R-31 – accounting for the extended jetpipes – but its airflow and weight would be compatible with the airframe of the MiG-25.

In theory, the Mach 2.4 top speed would make it feasible to build a lighter, more efficient aluminium-alloy structure, but the close likeness between the MiG-25 and MiG-31 makes it improbable that such a thing has been done. However, the MiG-31 is reported to have a stronger airframe than the MiG-25, lifting the older type's tight speed and manoeuvre limits at low altitude, and this may have been achieved at little cost in weight by substituting titanium alloys for steel. (Since the MiG-25 was designed, Soviet work in titanium has made great advances, and the Soviet Union is now the world's largest titanium producer.)

MiG-31 armament

The MiG-31's armament includes at least four air-to-air missiles of a new type, known to NATO as AA-9, mated to a new pulse-Doppler radar and fire-control system. Tests with the AA-9 were first observed in August 1977. According to US sources, the MiG-31 with the AA-9 has a true look-down/shoot-down capability, including the ability to intercept targets with an RCS of under 1m^2, at altitudes as low as 200ft (60m) above ground level, from a launch at 20,000ft (6,100m). In other tests, the system is reported to have engaged four larger targets – UR-1 supersonic drones, with a 5m^2 RCS – within 40sec, all at different altitudes; it has also intercepted a UR-1 at 70,000ft (21,300m), after a launch at 54,000ft (16,500m), demonstrating a 16,000ft (4,900m) 'snap-up' capability. In that test, the missile coasted to 125,000ft (38,000m) after passing close to the target. The missile has a range of 25-40nm (46-74km), and has its own active radar for guidance in the final stages of its flight, like the US Navy's AIM-54 Phoenix.

The significance of this information – which US intelligence apparently acquired by intercepting telemetered data during test firings – is that the MiG-31/AA-9 system can probably intercept any known aircraft, from an F-111 or B-1 in terrain-following flight to an SR-71 at its maximum altitude. Its capability against cruise missiles – which have a very small RCS, well below 1m^2 – is probably limited. The problem, in that case, is that the range and resolution of the missile's active terminal homing radar is limited by its antenna size. For the same reason, the system will have to be modified to cope with the forthcoming 'stealth' Advanced Technology Bomber.

Given its performance, the AA-9 is probably a large missile by Western standards; it may be in the same size class as the AA-7. The DoD credits the MiG-31 with the ability to carry eight missiles, but it is likely that this would be a mixed load, with four AA-9s on the wing pylons and four smaller missiles, on twin launchers, on the under-fuselage

Above: The 'Mainstay' AEW&C aircraft, based on the Il-76 freighter, goes hand in hand with the MiG-31. The interceptor, in fact, was designed as the best possible operational complement to the AEW&C aircraft.

pylons. The DoD-released impression also shows a pair of 440gal (2,000lit) fuel tanks on the outer pylons, which presumably. displace a pair of missiles. The MiG-31 is reported to carry an internal gun, probably in the lower fuselge.

Adding up the stretched fuselage, the corresponding increase in internal fuel capacity, the second crew station and the increased external load, it quickly becomes apparent that the MiG-31 is a big aeroplane, much heavier than any Western fighter (its empty weight is equivalent to the all-up weight of an F-15 with missiles and some external fuel).

The cancellation of the original B-1A production contract in June 1977 did not materially affect the MiG-31 programme. Development of the new bomber continued, and the production programme could have been reinstated at any time. This happened in October 1981, by which time the design had been significantly improved.

The MiG-31 is believed to have become operational in late 1982, and, even though its shape dates back a quarter of a century, it is a very potent combat aircraft and poses some serious problems for NATO. Unlike recent Western air-defence types, the MiG-31 is not compromised in the least for close-in combat: its wing loading and thrust/weight ratio clearly rule it out of the air-superiority envelope.

From its MiG-25 ancestor, the MiG-31 inherits an airframe that runs into no real limits at high speed and high altitude. The aerodynamic design is optimized for low supersonic drag, with few compromises. Its turbojet engines are sized for straight-and-level flight, rather than manoeuvre, and are more efficient at high Mach than turbofans.

The result is that the MiG-31 is a very honest Mach 2.4 aircraft. It should be able to attain Mach 2.4 even with four large missiles under its wings, and, because of its better-matched engines and large internal fuel capacity, it will have a greater supersonic endurance than in-service Western types. It operates routinely above 70,000ft (21,300m), well above the normal operating ceiling of any Western fighter.

With plenty of fuel and a reasonably efficient powerplant, the 800nm (1,500km) interception radius quoted by the DoD is probably realistic. This represents a mixed subsonic/supersonic mission with external fuel, and only a short burst of supersonic combat; however, it translates into the ability to cover a large area of the Soviet Union against a subsonic target such as a B-1, given accurate guidance by 'Mainstay' AEW&C aircraft to the target area. Alternatively, and unlike any other Soviet or Western fighter, the big MiG-31 can dash 400nm (750km) to the target area at Mach 2.4.

In the tactical theatre, the MiG-31/ 'Mainstay' combination poses a definite threat to Western deep-interdiction aircraft, which have up to now been fairly safe at low altitude; the smaller MiG-29 and Su-27 fighters do the same. The unique threat from the MiG-31, though, is directed at NATO assets such as the vital E-3 Awacs, and the increasing number of stand-off reconnaissance and control platforms. Operating at high speed and high altitude, the MiG-31 can make snap-down missile attacks against these vulnerable targets with very little warning. While the type is certainly not immune to interception, it operates close to the limits of most Western systems, and interception becomes considerably more difficult under such circumstances.

Interceptor deployment

With the advent of the MiG-31 and 'Mainstay', the re-equipment and re-organization of the Soviet interceptor force is nearing completion. Re-equipment of the air defence force has, so far, proceeded in two phases. A first, interim stage was represented by the arrival of MiG-23M 'Flogger-B/G' fighters, originally developed for tactical use but possessing at least some capability against low-flying targets, and the retrofit of the 'High Lark'/AA-7 missile system to the MiG-25 fleet. The MiG-31 and the 'Mainstay' constitute the second stage of improvement.

Meanwhile, the former IA-PVO (Interceptors of National Air Defence) force has been separated into two parts. More than half the pre-1980 force has been transferred to the VVS (Soviet Air Forces), and re-assigned to a generic point defence role under the local joint-services command. The entire fleet of Su-15s – the most modern interceptors in the world in 1972 – has been transferred to this force, along with other older types. A numerically smaller, better equipped core, dedicated to strategic air defence, still functions as part of the National Air Defence Troops (Voyska-PVO), and it is this force that will, increasingly, standardize on the MiG-31 and, possibly, more advanced aircraft.

The MiG-31 is, unquestionably, one of the world's best interceptors, and is one of the few aircraft that represent a problem for the B-1. Its development represents an economical use of an old airframe in a new role: a lesson which the West might do well to study.

Below: The importance of the new MiG-31 'Foxhound' in the modernization of Soviet air defences is graphically illustrated in this DoD projection of Soviet interceptor radar capability.

	1978	1983	1988 estimate
100%	FLOGGER B	FOXHOUND	100%
		FLOGGER B FLOGGER G FOXBAT E	
	FRESCO FARMER FISHPOT FIREBAR FIDDLER FLAGON FOXBAT		FLOGGER B FLOGGER G FOXBAT E
		FIREBAR FIDDLER FLAGON	
			FLAGON

Range only radar / Limited lookdown / True lookdown/ shootdown

Specifications

Mikoyan MiG-21F 'Fishbed-C'

Dimensions			Definition
	Span	23ft 6in/7.16m	
	Length overall	51ft 4in/15.65m	
	Length exc probe	44ft 2in/13.46m	
	Height	14ft 9in/4.5m	
	Wing area	247sq ft/22.9m^2	
Powerplant		One Tumansky R-11F turbojet	
	Thrust (dry)	9,500lb/42.2kN	
	Thrust (augmented)	12,650lb/56.2kN	
	Internal fuel	540Imp gal/2,470lit	
Weights	Empty	11,000lb/4,980kg	
	Normal take-off	16,250lb/7,370kg	Clean
	Max take-off	19,025lb/8,630kg	2 AAM, 1 × 108Imp gal/490lit tank
	Wing loading	77lb/sq ft/375kg/m^2	
Performance	Max speed	1,150kt/2,125km/h (Mach 2)	
	Max sea level speed	590kt/1,100km/h	
	Initial climb rate	25,900ft/min/132m/sec	
	Combat radius	120nm/220km	4 AAM, 1 tank
Armament	One or two internal 30mm NR-30 cannon; two wing hardpoints for AA-2 'Atoll' AAMs; centreline pylon for drop tank.		

Above: Combining a radar nose with the fin of the original 'Fishbed-A', this is probably the Ye-7 prototype for the entire MiG-21PF series.

Mikoyan MiG-21Mbis 'Fishbed-N'

Dimensions			Definition
	Span	23ft 6in/7.16m	
	Length overall	51ft 4in/15.65m	
	Length exc probe	47ft 11in/14.16m	
	Height	14ft 9in/4.5m	
	Wing area	247sq ft/22.9m^2	
Powerplant		One Tumansky R-25 turbojet	
	Thrust (dry)	13,000lb/57.8kN	
	Thrust (augmented)	19,850lb/88.2kN	
	Internal fuel	640Imp gal/2,900lit	
Weights	Empty	13,500lb/6,200kg	
	Normal take-off	19,300lb/8,750kg	2 AAM, 1 × 108Imp gal/490lit tank
	Max take-off	22,000lb/10,000kg	2 AAM, 3 tanks
	Wing loading	89lb/sq ft/435kg/m^2	
Performance	Max speed	1,200kt/2,230km/h (Mach 2.1)	
	Max sea level speed	Just over Mach 1	
	Initial climb rate	58,000ft/min/284m/sec	
	Combat radius	175nm/320km	4 AAM, 1 tank
Armament	One internal 23mm GSh-23 cannon; four wing hardpoints for up to 3,300lb (1,500kg) ordnance, inc. AA-2, AA-8, AS-7, rockets or bombs; centreline and outboard wing pylons for drop tanks.		

Above: Close-up of a MiG-21Mbis 'Fishbed-N', showing the panels which give access to control runs and fuzes. The large ground service connectors visible on the fuselage beneath the wing root are clearly designed with gloved hands and the rigours of Siberian weather in mind.

Above: This sequence shows the sometimes confusing changes of spine shape in the later MiG-21s. The narrow, straight-topped spine on the MiG-21MF 'Fishbed-J' (top) was introduced in the MiG-21PFMA. The MiG-21SMT 'Fishbed-K' (centre) has a very fat spine with a curved top line, ending in a mould line running across the entire chord of the fin. Finally, the MiG-21bis 'Fishbed-L' has a spine shape much closer to that of the MiG-21MF, but still fatter than that of the older aircraft; note downward curve of spine/fuselage junction, and the longer 'crease' where spine merges into fin.

Mikoyan MiG-23MF 'Flogger-G'

Dimensions			Definition
	Span (wings spread)	46ft 9in/14.25m	
	Span (wings swept)	27ft 2in/8.3m	
	Length overall	59ft 10in/18.25m	
	Length exc probe	55ft 6in/16.9m	
	Height	14ft 4in/4.35m	
	Wing area	325sq ft/30.2m^2	
Powerplant		One Tumansky R-29B turbojet	
	Thrust (dry)	17,500lb/78kN	
	Thrust (augmented)	25,350lb/113kN	
	Internal fuel	1,270Imp gal/5,750lit	
Weights	Empty	25,000lb/11,500kg	
	Normal take-off	38,000lb/17,250kg	
	Max take-off	42,500lb/19,250kg	6 AAM, 3 × 175Imp gal/800lit tanks
	Wing loading	130lb/sq ft/635kg/m^2	
Performance	Max speed	1,350kt/2,500km/h (Mach 2.35)	
	Max sea level speed	730kt/1,350km/h (Mach 1.1)	
	Combat radius	500nm/930km	4 AAM, 3 tanks
Armament	One twin-barrel 23mm GSh-23 cannon in lower fuselage; two medium-range R-23 (AA-7 'Apex') or four short-range R-60 (AA-8 'Aphid') on glove pylons, plus two or four R-60s under intake ducts.		

Above: A MiG-23MF 'Flogger-G' in dirty condition on the approach. Inevitably a more complex aircraft than the MiG-21, the MiG-23 is nevertheless markedly less so than its Western contemporaries.

Mikoyan MiG-27 'Flogger-J'

Dimensions	Span (spread)	46ft 9in/14.25m	
	Span (swept)	27ft 2in/8.3m	
	Length overall	58ft 1in/17.7m	
	Length exc probe	54ft 10in/16.72m	
	Height	14ft 4in/4.35m	
	Wing area	325sq ft/30.2m²	
Powerplant		One Tumansky R-29-300 turbojet	
	Thrust (dry)	17,500lb/78kN	
	Thrust (augmented)	25,350lb/113kN	
	Internal fuel	1,270Imp gal/5,750lit	**Definition**
Weights	Empty	25,000lb/11,500kg	
	Normal take-off	41,000lb/18,500kg	6,000lb stores
	Overload take-off	44,500lb/20,200kg	6,000lb/2,700kg stores, 2×175Imp gal/800lit tanks
	Wing loading	137lb/sq ft/670kg/m²	
Performance	Max speed	980kt/1,820km/h (Mach 1.7)	
	Max sea level speed	730kt/1,350km/h (Mach 1.1)	
	Combat radius	500nm/930km	6,000lb, 3 tanks
Armament	One six-barrel 23mm cannon, movable in elevation, in lower fuselage; up to 10,000lb (4,500kg) of stores under inlet ducts, wing gloves and rear fuselage. Options include: free-fall bombs on multiple racks, expendable decoy pods on rear fuselage; up to four AS-7 (radio command), AS-10 (laser-homing) or AS-12 ASMs; two AS-9 anti-radiation missiles; TV/laser-guided bombs; gun pods.		

Above: A murky but interesting shot of a MiG-27 'Flogger-J', showing its small leading edge root extensions. This aircraft is believed to be carrying a laser-guided bomb beneath the nearer inlet duct, and what may be an associated tracker/designator pod beneath the fuselage.

Mikoyan MiG-25 'Foxbat-A'

Dimensions	Span	46ft/14m	
	Length overall	74ft 10in/22.8m	
	Length exc probe	71ft 4in/21.75m	
	Height	18ft 5in/5.60m	
	Wing area	730sq ft/68m²	
Powerplant		Two Tumansky R-31 turbojets	
	Thrust (dry)	20,500lb/91kN	
	Thrust (augmented)	27,120lb/120.5kN	
	Internal fuel	3,900Imp gal/17,800lit	**Definition**
Weights	Empty	44,000lb/20,000kg	
	Max take-off	82,500lb/37,500kg	4 AA-6
	Wing loading	113lb/sq ft/550kg/m²	
Performance	Max speed	1,6250kt/3,010km/h (Mach 2.82)	
	Service ceiling	78,000ft/24,000m	2 AA-6 or 4 AA-7
	Initial climb rate	41,000ft/min/208m/sec	
	Interception radius	160nm/300km at Mach 2.8	
Armament	Four AA-6 'Acrid' or, on 'Foxbat-E', R-23 (AA-7 'Apex') AAMs.		

Left: MiG-25Rs. The 'Foxbat-B' (right) has some unusual features, such as modified upper and lower inlet lips and a small fairing alongside the inlet. In the rear is a 'Foxbat-D' fitted with side-looking airborne radar.

Above: This view of a MiG-25R 'Foxbat-B' shows the transparencies for long-focus oblique and vertical cameras, and the dielectric panels covering Doppler navigation equipment and electronic sensors.

Mikoyan MiG-29 'Fulcrum-A'

Dimensions	Span	39ft 6in/12m	
	Length overall	59ft/18m	
	Length exc probe	57ft/17.4m	
	Height	16ft 6in/5m	
	Wing area	450sq ft/42m²	
Powerplant		Two Tumansky R-33D turbofans	
	Thrust (dry)	11,250lb/50kN	
	Thrust (augmented)	18,300lb/81.3kN	
	Internal fuel	1,500Imp gal/6,750lit	
			Definition
Weights	Empty	22,500lb/10,200kg	
	Normal take-off	37,000lb/16,750kg	6 AAM, int fuel
	Max take-off	41,500lb/18,800kg	6 AAM, 3×175Imp
	Wing loading	92lb/sq ft/450kg/m²	gal/800lit tanks
Performance	Max speed	1,320kt/2,450km/h (Mach 2.3)	
	Max sea level speed	730kt/1,350km/h (Mach 1.1)	
	Combat radius	350nm/650km	6 AAM, 3 tanks
Armament	Internal cannon armament, possibly comprising two 30mm single-barrel weapons in Lerxes; wing and belly pylons for two R-23 plus four R-60 or four to six AA-10 air-to-air missiles.		

Mikoyan MiG-31 'Foxhound-A'

Dimensions	Span	46ft/14m	
	Length overall	75ft 8in/23m	
	Length exc probe	72ft 6in/22.14m	
	Height	18ft 5in/5.6m	
	Wing area	730sq ft/68m²	
Powerplant		Two Tumansky RD-F turbojets	
	Thrust (dry)	22,000lb/98kN	
	Thrust (augmented)	32,000lb/142.5kN	
	Internal fuel	4,100Imp gal/18,800lit	**Definition**
Weights	Empty	47,500lb/21,500kg	
	Max take-off	90,500lb/41,000kg	4 AA-9, 2×440Imp
	Wing loading	125lb/sq ft/600kg/m²	gal/2,000lit tanks
Performance	Max speed	1,385kt/2,560km/h (Mach 2.4)	
	Service ceiling	75,000ft/23,000m	
	Initial climb rate	41,000ft/min/208m/sec	
	Interception radius	800nm/1,500km	Subsonic cruise, 100nm/185km supersonic dash
		400nm/740km	Mach 2.4 dash
Armament	Four AA-9 air-to-air missiles, plus four smaller weapons.		

Picture credits

PRINTED IN BELGIUM BY proost INTERNATIONAL BOOK PRODUCTION